DE
FIGURIS
VENERIS

MANUAL OF CLASSICAL EROTOLOGY

by

FRED. CHAS. FORBERG

NEW YORK, 1964
MEDICAL PRESS OF NEW YORK

Printed in the United States of America

THE

Metamorphoses of Venus

E propose to pass in review the different metamorphoses of Venus, —
though truly not all of them. For
how is it possible to specify the
thousand modes (1), the thousand forms of

---

(1) Ovid, *Art of Love,* I, 435, 36: "To fully expose
the ungodly wiles of harlots, ten mouths, and as many
tongues to boot would not suffice."

Aloysia Sigea: "The body in sacrificing to Venus can
take as many postures as there are ways in which it can
bend and curve. It is equally impossible to enumerate all
these, as it is to say which is best fitted to give pleasure.
Each acts in this respect according to his own caprice,
according to place, time, and so on, choosing the one he
prefers. Love is not identical for each and all." (Dialogue VI.)

Love, on which the inventive satiety of pleasure ventures? But at any rate such as fall into distinct and definite kinds admit of being easily and methodically classified. Do not, inquisitive reader, hope for more than this. We are not of those who seek after a petty personal glory by unveiling the results of their own experience or by describing novel *tours de force* in the wrestling-school; we are not so much as raw recruits at this game. Nor yet is it our intention to reveal things we have seen or heard in this connexion. If we *would,* we could not,—to your satisfaction, for books are our only authorities. We are solely and entirely bookmen, and scarce frequent our fellow creatures at all.

These trifles engaged our attention first as a mere pastime. We were led to them accidentally, as we roamed from subject to subject for Philosophy, the garden we had hoped to set up our tent in for life, lies desolate. How *can* Philosophy flourish in times like ours, when almost every new day sees new systems sprout forth, to die down again tomorrow; when there are as many philosophers as philosophies, when schools have ceased to exist, when instead of groups only individuals are to be met with? Our second motive was to provide some satisfaction, however little, to the claims of those readers who very often find themselves disconcerted by the unconventional raciness of Ancient authors and their out-spoken witticisms, and justly complain of the prudish brevity or entire silence of the Commentators who leave their difficulties unexplained. Of course these latter wrote for the young; and no one can blame them under the circumstances for not having dwelt carefully and curiously on shameful secrets.

If we have fallen into any mistakes, lay the fault, we beg, first on our insufficient intellectual furniture, secondly on our ignorance as to the more uncommon forms of lust, an ignorance prevalent in small towns, and lastly, if you please, put it down to the honest simplicity of our Coburg citizens' *members*.

We only follow others' example. We have predecessors in Astyanassa, who according to Suidas (2) first wrote "of Erotic Postures";

---

(2) Suidas under *Astyanassa*: "Astyanassa, maid of Helen the wife of Menelaus, who was the first to invent the different positions in the act of love. She wrote "Of Erotic Postures"; and was followed and imitated by Phi-

and in Philaenis of Samos (3), or rather, to deprive no one of his due, Polycrates, an Athenian sophist, who brought out under the name of an honourable matron a book "On the various Postures of Love". Then there was Elephantis (4) or Elephantiné, a Greek girl,

---

laenis and Elephantine, who carried further the series of suchlike obscenities".

(3) *Priapeia,* LXIII: "To her a certain girl (I very nearly gave her name) is wont to come with her paramour; and if she fails to discover as many postures as Philaenis describes, she goes away again still itching with desire".

Philaenis has found a champion of her good name in Aeschrion, who wrote an epitaph for her that is still extant in Athenaeus, bk. VIII. ch. 13: The last lines read: "I was not lustful for men nor a gad-about; but Polycrates, by race an Athenian, a mill clapper of talk, a foul-tongued sophist, wrote—what he wrote; I know nought of it all".

Her works were familiar to Timarchus in Lucian (*Apophras,* p. 158,—vol. VII, of Works of Lucian, edit. J. P. Schmid: "Tell me where you find these words and expressions,—in what books? is it in the volumes of Philaenis, that are always in your hands?"

(4) Suetonius, *Tiberius,* ch. 43: "He decorated his various and variously arranged sleeping-chambers with pictures and bas-reliefs of the most licentious character, and furnished them with the works of Philaenis, that no one in performing should want a model of the posture required."

Priapeia, III: "Taking pictures from the licentious treatises of Elephantis, Lalagé presents them an offering

whose licentious writings Tiberius is said to
have furnished his sleeping-room with; also
Paxamus (5) who composed the *Dodecatech-*

---

to the stiff-standing god, and begs you prove if she per-
forms agreeably to the pictured postures."

It would seem then that artists depicted the postures
described by Elephantis, she herself possibly setting the
example. Paintings of the sort Lalagé dedicates to Priapus, and asks her lover to have her and see if she is a do-
cile pupil in faithfully imitating all the modes of connection depicted in them. No doubt such representations
of licentious postures, taken from the works of Elephantis
or Philaenis or elsewhere stimulated the ingenuity of
Artists to work out in emulation these enticing *motifs* to
the highest degree of finish. *Ovid* alludes to such works
of art in his *Art of Love,* II, 680: "They unite in Love
in a thousand postures; no picture could suggest any fresh
ones..."; as also the author of an ancient Epigram quoted
by *Joseph Scaliger* in his Commentary on the *Priapeia,*
III; "And when she has thrown herself into every posture in imitation of the seductive pictures, she may go:
but let the picture be left hanging over my bed." Nothing
was commoner with the Romans than to decorate the wall
and partitions of rooms with licentious paintings, as may
be gathered from Propertius II, vi, 27 sqq.: "The hand
that first painted filthy pictures, and exposed foul sights
in an honest home, corrupted the pure eyes of young
maids, and chose to make them accomplices of his own
lubricity. In old days our walls were not daubed with
fancies of this vile sort, when never a partition was
adorned with a vicious subject."

(5) *Suidas*: "Paxamus wrote the *Dodecatechmon;* the
subject is the obscene postures." But I think he has no
good reason to connect with this the epithet *Dodecame-*

non on lascivious postures; and Sotades (6)

---

chanos given to a certain Cyrené. The said wanton damsel seems to have practised rather than described the twelve postures of Venus. *Suidas* under *Dodecamechanon*: "There was a famous *hetaera*, Cyrené by name, further known as *Dodecamechanos*, because she practised twelve different postures in making love".

Aristophanes says in the *Frogs*, 1361-63: "Do you dare to criticize my songs, you that modulate your cadences on the twelve-fold postures of Cyrené?". Her name occurs also in the *Thesmophoriazusae* (104), but merely her name. (Our invariable rule is to quote from Burmann's edition of Aristophanes.) I am doubtful as to whether Musaeus should be counted among writers on the Erotic postures. Martial (XII, 97) recommends Instantius Rufus to read his (Musaeus') books, as being of the most advanced laciviousness, vying with those of the Sybarites in obscenity and full of the most suggestive and spicy wit; warning him at the same time to have his girl ready to hand, if he did not want his hands to perform the wedding-march and consummate the marriage without a woman at all.

(6) *Athenaeus,* XIV, 13: "Also the Ionic dialect has to show the poems of Sotades and the "Ionic" poems preceding his, those of Alexander the Aetolian, and Pyres of Miletus, and Alexis, and others of the same class. The last mentioned is known as the Cinaedologue. But in this *genre* the most eminent writer is Sotades, of Maroneia, as is stated by Carystius of Pergamus in his work on Sotades, and by Apollonius, Sotades' son, who also wrote a work on his father's poems. "His end was a miserable one. Having assailed Ptolemy Philadelphus, king of Egypt, with witticisms too independent for the sensitive ears of princes, the king caused him to be enclosed in a leaden casket, and thrown into the sea."

of Maroneia, surnamed the Cinaedologue, from whose name a whole class of literature, remarkable for its excessive lubricity, is known as the Sotadic; and Sabellus, of whom Martial speaks: "Copious verses, only too copious, on scandalous subjects you have read me, O Sabellus, such as neither the maids of Didymus (7) know, nor yet the wanton treatises of Elephantis. Therein are new postures of Love that the desperate fornicator tries, and what debauchees use, but never tell of,—how grouped in a series five copulate at once, how a greater number still can make a chain. It was hardly worth the pains to be erudite".

Moreover amongst our predecessors was

---

(7) Who were these "maids of Didymus". Nobody knows. Failing any more plausible supposition, it may very well be conjectured that among the four thousand works written according to Seneca (Letter LXXXVIII) by the Grammarian Didymus, there was one on the postures of lascivious girls, worthy to be named side by side with the treatises of Elephantis. Undoubtedly a man who devoted himelf to such subtle questions as whether Anacreon was more libertine than drunkard, whether Sappho was a public woman or not, was quite likely to discuss the Erotic postures.

the famous Pietro Aretino (8), a man of an almost divine genius, whom ill-natured report represents as having illustrated sixteen plates painted by Julio Romano and engraved on copper by Marc-Antonio with verses indecent beyond all expression; Lorenzo Veniero again (9), a Venetian nobleman, author of a little

---

(8) See *Bayle's* Dictionary, article: *Pierre Arétin;* also Murr's *Journal zur Kunstgeschichte* (Year-Book of the History of Art), vol. XIV, pp. 1-72.

(9) *Pierre Bayle,* in his Dictionary, under *Pierre Arétin*: "There is a *Dialogue between Maddalena and Giula,* entitled *La Puttana Errante* (The wandering whore), in which are exhaustively treated *i diversi congiungimenti* (the different modes of intercourse), to the number of thirty-five. Aretino, though the book has always been printed under his name, disowns it, declaring it to be the work of one of his pupils named Veniero." *Brunet,* Manual du Libraire (Book dealer's Handbook). "The *Puttana errante,* a little book, very rare, quite worthy of Aretino in view of the obscenities it countains, but which has been erroneously attributed to him. Lorenzo Veniero, a Venetian nobleman, is the real author. He published it to avenge himself on a Venetian courtesan named Angela, whom he designates under the insulting name of Zaffetta, that is to say, in the Venetian dialect, daughter of a police-spy."

[*Bayle, Forberg* and many other writers have confused the *Puttana errante,* a poem by Lorenzo Veniero and a burlesque parody of the Romances of chivalry, with the *Dialogue between Maddalena and Giulia,* a prose work to which the Elzevirs gave the title properly belonging to

work in Italian, bearing the title *La Puttana Errante* (The Wandering Whore), in which he has undertaken to specify no less than thirty-five modes of loving. Lastly there was Nicolas Chorier, a French lawyer, who under the name of Aloysia Sigaea, a young Spanish lady, has given us the *Satirae Sotadicae de arcanis Amoris et Veneris* (Sotadic Satires on the Secret Rites of Love and Venus); though the book also appears under the name of Joannes Meursius with the title *Elegantiae Latini Sermonis* (Graces of Latin Prose). In this book you do not know which to admire most, the style at once elegant, correct and careful, yet free from pedantry, the wit equally gay and graceful, the brilliant sparks of Latin erudition that glitter everywhere, the rich and copious eloquence graced as with jewels by polished and luminous words and phrases of a pleasant antique flavour, or lastly the pre-emi-

---

the poem. Neither one nor the other is the work of Pietro Aretino. See note at end of vol. VI. of the *Dialogues du divin Pietro Aretino* (Dialogues of the divine Pietro Aretino), Paris, Liseux, 1879, 3 vols. 18°, and London, 1880, 3 vols. 18°. [Note of French Translation of Forberg, *Manuel d'Erotologie classique,* Paris Liseux, 1882.]

nent skill displayed in varying with such manifold versatility one simple theme. The others we need not mention further.

Our predecessors, whether the more modern, or those of Antiquity whom we have cited, and all whose works alas! envious time has robbed us of, did not lack severe critics, nor yet studious readers. And our own treatise will no doubt in its turn meet with both these classes. It is a man's book; we have written it, fearless of censure, for men,—not for such as are wont with growning brow "to pitchfork nature out of doors", but rather for such as have once for all dared to live their lives, who neither wish to lurk in darkness nor yet to defy the open day with effrontery, in one word for those who think that in Love as in all else the golden mean is the course to choose. Let others go their way, and arrogate to themselves the title of sages!

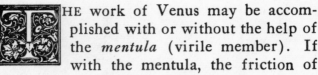HE work of Venus may be accomplished with or without the help of the *mentula* (virile member). If with the mentula, the friction of this organ, in which friction the whole pleasure consists, can be effected either in the *vulva* (female organ), in the *anus* (arse-hole), in the mouth, by the hand or in any cavity of the body. If without the mentula, the vulva may be worked either with the tongue, with the clitoris, or with any object resembling the virile organ.

CHAPTER I

OF COPULATION

AND first of all let us consider what is accomplished by means of the mentula introduced into the vulva. This is, properly speaking, to effect copulation; but there are various ways of doing it. As a matter of fact copulation can be effected: —the man face downwards with the woman on her back, the man on his back with the woman face down, the man on his back with the woman turning her back to him; the man sitting with the woman turning her face towards him, sitting with the woman turning her back to him; the man standing or kneeling with the woman turning her face towards him, standing or kneeling with the woman turning her back to him. Let us examine each of these methods separately.

Coition with the man face down on the woman who lies on her back is the ordinary method, and the most natural.

Aloysia Sigaea says:

"For my own part I like the usual custom and the ordinary method best: the man should lie upon the woman, who is on her back, breast to breast, stomach to stomach, pubis to pubis, piercing her tender cleft with his rigid spear. Indeed what can be imagined sweeter than for the woman to lie extended on her back, bearing the welcome weight of her lovers' body, and exciting him to the tender transports of a restless but delicious voluptuousness? What more pleasant than to feast on her lovers' face, his kisses, his sighs, and the fire of his wanton eyes? What better than to press the loved one in her arms and so awake new fires of desire, to participate in amorous sensations unblunted by any taint of age or infirmity? What more favorable to the delight and enjoyment of both than such lascivious movements given and received? What more opportune at the instant of dying a voluptious death than to recover again under the revivifying vigour of burning kisses? He who plies Venus on the reverse side, satisfies but one of his senses, he who does the same face to face satisfied them all". (Dialogue VI.)

Ovid, the Master of Loves' Mysteries, invites pretty women to take this posture by preference:

"See you reckon up each of your charms, and take your posture according to your beauty. One and the same mode does not become every woman. You are especially attractive of face; then lie on your back." (*Art of Love*, III, 771-773.)

This posture is by no means limited to one mode. The woman lying on her back, the rider may clasp her between his legs, or she may receive him between hers. Yet another position may be adopted, according as the woman lie back with legs stretched wide apart or with the knees raised.

It is this position,—lying on her back with legs wide apart, that Caviceo asks Olympia to assume for making Love:

"I do not wish you", he says, "to work your buttocks, or to respond with corresponding movements to my efforts. Neither do I wish you to lift your legs up, whether both at once, or one after the other, when I have mounted you. What I do wish you to do is this: First stretch your thighs as far apart, open them as wide as a woman well can. Offer your vulva to the member which is going to pierce it, and without altering this position, let *me* complete the work... Count my thrusts one by one, and see you make no mistake in the total" (Aloysia Sigaea, Dialogue V).

Would you see a representation of this? Take the tale *Félicia ou mes fredaines,* part II, chap. xxv, and look at the plate facing the text.

The other position, in which the woman is lying with her knees raised, is the one which Callias makes Tullia take:

"After I am lying upon your dear body", he says, "press me fast in your arms, and hold me thus embraced. Draw your legs back as far as you can, so that your pretty feet touch your buttocks, smooth as marble" (Aloysia Sigaea, Dialogue VI).

If you would enter the woman lying on her back with her legs in the air, it may be done in yet another way than Tullia's mode, and one perhaps still more delicious, by placing your mistress so that she rests her legs crossed over the loins of her rider. A representation of this very pleasant posture, which would rouse the numbed tool of a Hippolytus, is to be found in part IV. of the *Félicia* mentioned above. There is another similar plate in chap. xxi, not without charm. Doris, in the epigram of Sosipater, vol. I. of the *Analecta* of Brunck (p. 584), seems also to have made a trial of this figure:

"When I stretched Doris with the rosy buttocks on the bed, I felt immortal in my youthful vigour; for she clipped me round the middle with her strong legs, and unswervingly rode out the long-course of Love."

Doris did not bestride him; the expression, "When I stretched" shows this; she was lying on her back, and with her feet lifted up clasped her rider.

But again the feet of the woman lying on her back may also be held up by others. In this way Aloysio enjoyed Tullia with the help of Fabrizio, in the VI. Dialogue of Aloysia Sigaea, where Tullia expresses herself as follows:

"Aloysio and Fabrizio come running towards me. "Lift up your legs", says Aloysio to me, threatening me with his cutlas. I lifted them up. Then down he lies on my bosom, and plunges his cutlass in my ever open wound. Fabrizio raised my two legs in the air, and slipping a hand under each of my hams, moves my loins for me without any trouble on my part. What a singular and pleasant mode of making you move! I declared I was on fire, but before I could end my sentence, the overflowing foam of Venus quenched the fire (10)".

So too was it with feet in air, whether of her own accord or seconded by another, that Leda gave herself, with her husband's consent, to the doctors who had been called in, as Martial describes the scene:

---

(10) This method was not unknown at the time of Aristophanes, as we see from the following passage of the *Peace*:

"So that you may straightway, lifting up the girl's legs, accomplish high in air the mysteries" (v. 889, 890).

And in the *Birds* he says:

"For this girl, your first messenger, why! I will lift up her legs and will in between her thighs" (v. 1254, 55).

"To her old spouse Leda had declared herself to be hysterical, and complains she must needs be f...cked; yet with tears and groans avers she will not buy health at such a price, and swears she had rather die. The husband beseeches her to live, not to die in her youth and beauty; and permits others to do what he cannot effect himself. Straightway the doctors arrive, the matrons retire; and up go the wife's legs in air; oh! medicine grave and stern!" (XI, 72.)

Face downwards to her the man may do the woman's business, while she is half reclining, either obliquely in bed, or on a chair, or lying sideways.

The latter position is recommended by Ovid to the woman with rounded thighs and faultless figure:

"She that has young rounded thigh and flawless bosom, should ever lie reclined sideways on the couch" (11) (*Art of Love,* II, v. 781, 782).

---

(11) Readers will find another figure given in some of the books: "The man should be standing, while the woman reclines sideways on the bed."

Copulation face to face with the woman sitting obliquely is described by Aloysia Sigaea with her usual elegance and vivacity:

"Caviceo came on, blithe and joyous" (it is Olympia speaking). He despoils me of my chemise, and his libertine hand touches my parts. He tells me to sit down again as I was seated before, and places a chair under either foot in a way that my legs were lifted high in air, and the gate of my garden was wide open to the assaults I was expecting. He then slides his right hand under my buttocks and draws me a little closer to him. With his left he supported the weight of his spear. Then he laid himself down on me... put his battering-ram to my gate, inserted the head of his member into the outermost fissure, opening the lips of it with his fingers. But there he stopped, and for awhile made no further attack. "Octavia sweetest", he says, "clasp me tightly, raise your right thigh and rest it on my side."—"I do not know what you want", I said. Hearing this he lifted my thigh with his own hand, and guided it round his loin, as he wished; finally he forced his arrow into the target of Venus. In the beginning he pushes in with gentle blows, then quicker, and at last with such force I could not doubt that I was in great danger. His member was hard as horn, and he forced it in so cruelly, that I cried out, "You will tear me to pieces." He stopped a moment from his work. "I implore you to be quiet, my dear", he said, "it can only be done this way; endure it without flinching". Again his hand slid under my buttocks, drawing me nearer, for I had made a feint to draw back, and without more delay plied me with such fast and furious blows that I was near fainting away. With a violent effort he forced his spear right in, and the point fixed itself in the depths of the wound. I cry out... Caviceo spurted out his venerean exudation, and I felt irrigated by a burning rain... Just as Caviceo slackened, I experienced a sort of voluptuous itch as though I were making water; involuntarily I draw my buttocks back a little, and in an instant I felt with supreme pleasure something flowing from me which tickled me deliciously. My eyes failed me, my breath came thick, my face was on fire, and I felt my whole body melting. "Ah! ah! ah! my Caviceo, I shall faint away", I cried; "hold my soul—it is escaping from my body" (Dialogue V).

Finally the conjunction with the woman lying on her side, particularly on her right side, is deemed by Ovid the most simple, calling for the least effort:

"A thousand modes of Love are there; the simplest and least laborious of all is when the woman lies reclined on her right side" (*Art of Love*, III, 787, 88).

Above all this position is the most convenient for tall women:

"Let her press the bed with her knees, with the neck slightly bowed, she whose chief beauty is her long shapely flank" (*Art of Love,* III, v. 779, 80).

It seems that the Phyllis of Martial allowed herself to be done in that way:

"Two arrived in the morning, who wanted to lie with Phyllis, and each was fain to be first to held her naked body in his arms; Phyllis promised to satisfy them both together, and she did it; one lifted her leg, the other her tunic" (X, 81).

She was lying on her side; the f... lifted her leg; the pederast her tunic.

We now come to the manner, in which the man lying on his back has connection with the woman face downwards. The parts are interchanged; the woman plays the rider and the man the horse. This figure was called the horse of Hector.

Martial says:

"Behind the doors the Phrygian slaves would be masturbating, every time Andromaché mounted her Hector horse fashion" (XI, 105).

Ovid, however, with much sagacity denies that this posture could have pleased Andromaché; her figure was too tall, for this to have been agreeable or even possible for her. It is for little women, that it is pleasant to be thus placed:

"A little woman may very well get astride on her horse; but tall and majestic as she was, the Theban bride never mounted the Hectorean horse" (*Art of Love* III, v. 777, 778).

It is no business of ours to decide the question.

At any rate Sempronia takes this posture with Crisogono.

"He could wait no longer: "Are you un-

dressed", said Cricogono. "Now, my Sempronia, take the position, which gives me so
much pleasure, you know which." He
stretches himself down on his back, she gets
upon him astride, with her face towards him,
and with her own hand guides his burning
arrow between her thighs" (Aloysia Sigea,
Dial. VII).

This is the same attitude, which in Horace
is imposed by the slave upon the little harlot,
who:

".....naked in the light of the lantern, plied
with wanton wiles and moving buttocks the
horse beneath her" (Sat. II. vii, v. 50).

As to the matron spoken of v. 64 of the same
satire as "never having sinned *above*", no
doubt this posture did not suit her. Women
have not all the same taste.

Evidently, it was as little to the taste of the
girl whom Xanthias in Aristophanes' *Wasps*
(v. 499) asked to ride him; for she asks him
indignantly, and playing on the double meaning of the word (Hippias and ——, a horse),
if he was for re - establishing Hippias'
tyranny: "Irritated she asked me if I wanted
to revive the tyranny of Hippias."

Again in his *Lysistrata* (v. 678) this master of wanton wit points to the same thing, declaring the female sex to be very good at riding and fond of driving: "Woman loves to get on horseback and to stick there."

Aristophanes mocks similarly those, of whom he says, in verse 60 of the same play, that "They are aboard their barks". "They are mounted on their chargers". For ———— signifies both a ship and a horse. Plango in Asclepiades, Brunck's *Analecta,* vol. I, 217, affects the same figure.

"When she in horsemanship vanquished the ardent Philaenis, whilst her Hesperian coursers foamed under her reins."

Yet more expert in this kind of amorous riding than Philaenis herself, this ardent votary of pleasure thanks Venus in this epigram, that she has been able so to exhaust certain Hesperian gallants, whom she had mounted, that they had left her with wanton members all drooping, and feeling no desire left in them. To bestride men was also the favourite pastime of Lysidicé, who was never tired in the service of Venus, of whom the following epigram of Asclepiades treats:

"Many a horse has she ridden beneath her, yet never galled her thigh with all her nimble movements."

Courtesans consecrated to Venus a whip, a bit, a spur, in order to signify, that with their clients they like best to pose themselves in that way, and that they preferred riding themselves to being ridden,—nothing more.

It is the same when in Apuleius, Fotis satiated her Lucius with the pleasures of the undulating Venus:

"Saying this she leaped upon the couch and, seated upon me backwards, plying her hips, vibrating her lithe spine lasciviously, she satiated me with the delights of the undulating Venus, till both of us exhausted, powerless and with useless limbs, sunk down, exhaling our souls in mutual embraces" (*Metamorph.*, II, ch. II).

The next figure,—the man lying supine and the woman turning her back to him, is executed by Rangoni with Ottavia, under the direction of Tullia:

RANGONI: Look how stiff I stand! But I want to try the bliss in a new way.

TULLIA: In a new way? No! I swear by

my wanton soul you shall not. You shall not take a new way.

RANGONI: It was a slip of the tongue; I meant to say a new posture.

TULLIA: And what sort of one? I have an idea... what they call the horse of Hector. Lie down on your back, Rangoni; let your puissant spear stand firm to the enemy, who is to be pierced, Well done!

OTTAVIA: What must I do, Tullia?

TULLIA: Clip Rangoni between your thighs, mounting him a-straddle. His cutlass as he lies should meet your sheath poised over it. Why! you've taken the position admirably. Excellent!

RANGONI: Oh! what a back, worthy of Venus! Oh! the ivory sides! Oh! the inviting buttocks!

TULLIA: No naughty words! He who praises the buttocks, slanders the vulva! You know better, Ottavia! Her greedy vulva has swallowed your bristling member whole, Rangoni.

OTTAVIA: Quick, Rangoni, it is coming!... quick, quick, help me!

RANGONI: I am coming, Ottavia,—I am

come! Are you?—Are you, darling!

TULLIA: How now? Are you so quickly
done up, you two? (Aloysia Sigaea, Dial.
VI).

The pygiacic (12) mysteries, to which Eumolpus in Petronius (Satires, ch, cxl), invites a young girl, refer to the posture practised by the man lying on his back, with the
woman upon him, her back turned towards
him.

"Eumolpus did not hesitate to invite the
young girl to the pygiacic mysteries, but
begged of her to seat herself upon the goodness known to her (that being himself, to
whose goodness the mother had recommended
her daughter), and ordered Corax to get on
his stomach under the bed on which he was,
so that with his hands pressed against the
floor, he might assist with his movements
those of his master. Corax obeyed, beginning
with slow undulations responding to those of
the young girl. When the crisis was ap-
proaching, Eumolpus exhorted Corax with a
loud voice to quicken up his movements.
Thus placed between his servant and his mis-

---

(12) From ——— buttock.

tress, the old man took his pleasure as in a swing."

Would it be surprising, if in these posterior mysteries, Eumolpus' member had perchance gone wrong, and taken by mistake one orifice for the other?

You will find this figure represented in a copper-plate engraving in the very elegant book of d'Hancarville, *Monuments du culte secret des dames romaines,* ch. xxv, and you will be glad to know the note, with which the learned annotator accompanies the same.

"This attitude is to the taste of many men, and even the ladies find an increase of pleasure in practising it. It is supposed, that Priapus penetrates farther in, and that the fair one by her movements procures for herself a more voluptuous delight, and a more abundant libation."

Is it possible for the man, conveniently, to manage the business while turning his back to the woman lying on her back? Experts must decide. Aloysia Sigaea says with good common sense:

"There are many postures it is impossible to execute, even supposing the joints and loins of the candidates for the sacred joys of Venus more flexible than can be believed. By dint of pondering and reflection more ideas occur to the fancy than it is practicable to realize: Nothing is inconceivable to the longings of an unbridled will; nothing difficult to a furious and unregulated imagination. Love will find out a way; and an ardent fancy level mountains. Only the body is unable to comply with everything the mind, good or bad, suggests."

In another work of d'Hancarville's, *Monuments de la vie privée des douze Césars,* plate XXVII, you find represented men seated and copulating with women, who are facing them; plate XV, in the same book presents to your curiosity a man sitting and working a woman, who turns her back on him. Augustus is seated: he is attacking backwards, with true imperial audacity, Terentia (13), the

---

(13) Dio Cassius, LIV, 19: "He was so fond of her, that one day he matched her against Livia, as to which of them was the most beautiful." It was no bad idea to engage them in such a match, but think you he suffered them to fight this out in any costume but that in which the Goddesses three presented themselves before the dazed eyes of Paris?

wife of Maecenas, after drawing her onto his lap; Maecenas is present, asleep—asleep of course only for the Emperor. You may see a similar posture in the *Contes et Nouvelles en vers* by Jean de la Fontaine: it is on the plate appended to the tale, called *Le Tableau,* p. 223, vol. II, Amsterdam, 1762.

Nothing is more frequent than conjunction whilst standing, the woman with her back to the man; it is indeed very easy to do it that way in any place, as you have only to lift up the fair one's petticoats, and out with your weapon; it is, therefore, the best manner for those who have to make instantaneous use of an opportunity, when it is important to be sharp about it, as may happen, when you take your pleasure in secret. Thus Priapus complains of the wives and daughters of his neighbors, who came incessantly to him burning with ticklish desires.

"Cut off my genital member, which every night and all night long my neighbours' wives and daughters, for ever and for ever in heat, more wanton than sparrows in springtide, tire to death,—or I shall burst!..." (*Priapeia,* XXV).

I remember a medical man of our time, one of the most celebrated professors, (I had nearly uttered his name), who to emphasize this, called his daughter, and pointing to the blushing girl, while his hearers could not help smiling said: "This girl I fabricated standing." A representation of this position is to be found in the *Monuments de la vie privée de douze Césars,* pl. XLVI, and another in the *Monuments du culte secrets des dames romaines,* pl. XIII.

But further, a man may join himself to a woman standing face to face by supporting her in such a way, that her whole body is lifted up, her thighs resting on the man's hips, os else by lifting up the lower part of her body, whilst the upper part is resting on a couch. Will you feast you eyes with a representation of this not ungraceful position? If so you will not omit to look at plate XXIV of the *Monuments du culte secret des dames romaines,* and plate XL of the *Monuments de la vie privée des douze Césars*; Ovid, if I am not mistaken, had his eyes on one or the other of these figures:

"Milanion was supporting Atalanta's legs

on his shoulders; if they are fine legs this is how they should be held" (*Art of Love,* III, vv. 775, 776). The former of these modes is no doubt that described by Aloysia Sigaea, Past Mistress of these naughtinesses, and with a vivacity, a grace, and elegance that leaves nothing to be desired:

"La Tour came forward instantly..... I had thrown myself on the foot of the bed"— (Tullia is speaking)—"I was naked; his member was erect. Without more ado he grasps in either hand one of my breasts, and brandishing his hard and inflamed lance between my thighs, exclaims "Look Madam, how this weapon is darting at you, not to kill you, but to give you the greatest possible pleasure. Pray, guide this blind applicant into the dark recess, so that it may not miss its destination; I will not remove my hands from where they are, I would not deprive them of the bliss they enjoy." I do as he wishes, I introduce myself the flaming dart into the burning centre; he feels it, drives in, pushes home... After one or two strokes I felt myself melting away with incredible titillation, and my knees all but gave way. "Stop",

I cried—"stop my soul, it is escaping!" "I know", he replied, laughing, "from where. No doubt your soul wants to escape through this lower orifice, of which I have possession; but I keep it well stoppered." Whilst speaking he endeavoured, by holding his breath, still further to increase the already enormous size of his swollen member. "I am going to thrust back your escaping soul", he added, poking me more and more violently. His sword pierced yet deeper into the quick. Redoubling his delicious blows, he filled me with transports of pleasure,—working so forcefully that, albeit he could not get his whole body into me, he impregnated me with all his passion, all his lascivious desires, his very thoughts, his whole delirious soul by his voluptuous embraces. At last feeling the approach of the ecstasy and the boiling over of the liquid, he slips his hands under my buttocks, and lifts me up bodily. I do my part; I twine my arms closely round his form, my thighs and legs being at the same time intertwisted and entangled with his, so that I found myself suspended on his neck in the air, lifted clean off the ground; I was thus hanging, as it were, fixed on a peg. I had not the patience to wait for him, as he was going on, and again I swooned with pleasure. In the most violent raptures I could not help crying out—"I feel all... I feel all the delights of Juno lying with Jupiter. I am in heaven." At this moment La Tour, pushed by Venus and Cupido to the acmé of voluptuousness, poured a plenteous flood of his well into the genial hold, burning like fire. The creeper does not cling more closely round the walnut tree than I hold fast to La Tour with my arms and legs" (Dial. VI).

As to the last manner by means of which copulation may be achieved, the man standing with the woman half lifted up, Conrad practises it with slight modifications.

(TULLIA speaking): "He opened my thighs—I do not dislike Conrad, though I am not particularly partial to him. I neither consented, nor refused. As to him, he fancied a novel posture, and not at all a bad one. I was lying on my back; he raised my right thigh on his shoulder, and in this position he transfixed me, while I was awaiting the event, without greatly desiring it. He had at the same time extended my left thigh along his right thigh. His tool plunged into the root, he began to push and poke, quicker and quicker. What need to say more? Picture the conclusion for yourself" (Dial. VI).

Last of all, a man can get into a woman turning her back to him after the manner of the quadrupeds, who can have no connection with their females otherwise than by mounting upon them from behind (14). Some authorities have held that a woman conceives easier while on all fours. Lucretius says:

"....Women are said to conceive more readily when down after the manner of beasts, as the organs can absorb the seed best so, when the bosom is depressed and the loins lifted" (*Of the Nature of Things,* IV, vv. 1259-1262).

Also Aloysia Sigaea:

"Some people pretend that the fashion to make love indicated by Nature is that one where the woman offers herself for copulation after the manner of the animals, bent down with the hips raised; the virile ploughshare

---

(14) Pliny has treated this at great length in his *Natural History* (Book X, ch. 63).

penetrates thus more conveniently into the female furrow, and the seminal flow waters the field of love... The doctors, however, are against this posture; they say it is incompatible with the conformation of the parts destined for generation". (Dial. VI.)

However this may be, it happens frequently, that women cannot be managed in any other way. Given an obese man and a woman likewise obese or with child, how are they to do the thing otherwise? This is the reason why, so they say, Augustus having married Livia Drusilla, divorced wife of Tiberius Nero and already six months gone in pregnancy, had connection with her after the manner of animals. Plate VII of the *Monuments de la vie privée des douze Césars* will give you an idea of the posture assumed by both of them. But why should we not give you the annotations whereby the learned editor has elucidated the plate? Here they are:

"This Drusilla was the famous Livia, the wife of Tiberius Nero, who had been one of Anthony's friends. Augustus fell violently in love with her, and Tiberius gave her up to him, although she was at the time six months with child. A good many jokes were made about the eagerness of the Emperor, and one day, while they were all at table, and Livia was reclining by Augustus, one of those naked children, whom matrons used to educate for their pleasures, going up to Livia said: "What are you doing here? yonder is your husband", pointing to Nero, "there he is" (15). Soon afterwards Livia was confined, and the Romans said openly, that lucky people get children three months after being married, which passed into a proverb. One historian says that Augustus was obliged to caress his wife "after the manner of beasts" on account of her pregnancy, and it was to this luxurious attitude that the cameo of Apollonius, the celebrated gem-cutter of the time of Augustus, makes allusion. True that the state in which Livia was may have made this posture necessary: but it seems that it was at all times to the taste of the Ancients, either because they considered this attitude favourable for procreation, as Lucretius maintains, or because they found it to be a refinement of voluptuousness. The most ex-

(15) Compare Dio Cassius, bk. XLVIII, ch. 44.

traordinary and least natural postures have always appeared to rakes as enhancing the pleasure of the conjunction. But it must be admitted that imagination still outruns actual possibilities."

A singular reason for the necessity of encountering a woman backwards is given by Aloysia Sigaea, with her usual sagacity:

"For pleasure, one likes a vulva which is not placed too far back, so as to be entirely hidden by the thighs; it should not be more than nine or ten inches from the navel. With the greater number of girls the pubis goes so far down, that it may easily be taken as the other way of pleasure. With such coition is difficult. Theodora Aspilqueta could not be deflowered, till she placed herself prone on her stomach, with her kness drawn up to her sides. Vainly had her husband tried to manage her, while lying on her back, he only lost his oil" (Dialogue VII).

Ovid recommends this way with women who begin to be wrinkled:

"Likewise you, whose stomach Lucina has marked with wrinkles, mount from behind, like the flying Parthian with his steed" (*Art of Love,* III, v. 785, 86).

The same advice also seems to be given by him a little before:

"Let them be seen from behind whose backs are sightly" (v. 774).

But besides necessity, it is a fact that women are worked in this way out of mere caprice, variety offering the greatest pleasure. It is simply for this reason that Tullia suffers Fabrizio to do her that way, in Aloysia Sigaea:

"As Aloisio got up" (Tullia speaks) "Fabrizio makes ready for another attack. His member is swollen up, red and threatening. "I beg of you "Madam", he says, "turn over on your face." I did as he wished. When he saw my buttocks, whiter than ivory and snow, "How beautiful you are!" he cried. "But raise yourself on your knees and bend your head down." I bow my head and bosom, and lift my buttocks. He thrust his swift-moving and fiery dart to the bottom of my vulva, and took one of my nipples in either hand. Then he began to work in and out, and soon sent a sweet rivulet into the cavity of Venus. I also felt unspeakable delight, and had nearly fainted with lust. A surprising quantity of seed secreted by Fabrizio's loins filled and delighted me; a similar flow of my own exhausted my forces. In that single assault I lost more vigour than in the three preceding ones" (Dialogue VI) (16).

This copulation from the back is practicable in another very pleasant fashion, an excellent reproduction of which can be seen in the *Monument du culte secret des dames romaines,* plate XXVIII. A woman is represented with her hands placed on the ground, while the lower part of the body is lifted up and suspended by cords; she is turning her back to the man who stands. This seems to be much the same position as was taken up by the wife of the artisan Apu-

---

(16) The thing itself is very old; Aristophanes alludes to it in the *Peace*:

"To wrestle on the ground, to stand on all fours" (v. 896).

And in the *Lysistrata*:

"I will not squat down like a lioness carved on a knife-handle" (v. 231).

leius speaks of in his *Metamorphoses* (book IX), whom "bending over her, the lover planed with his adze, while she leant forward over a cask". An engraving showing this ingenious attitude is appended to the story of *The Tub* in the *Contes et Nouvelles en vers* of Jean de La Fontaine, vol. II, p. 215.

CHAPTER II

ON PEDICATION

S O much for copulation in the normal way. We will now discuss another mode of pleasure,—that due to introduction of the member into the anus. A man who exercises his member in the anus, be it of a man or a woman, pedicates; he is called a pederast, pedicon, drawk (17), and the other party, who allows himself to be invaded in that way, is called the patient, cinaedus, catamite (18), minion,

(17) *Drawk,* from —, I work, execute; for *dravicus,* as *cautus* for *cavitus, lautus* for *lavitus.*

(18) Catamite according to Festus, is the same thing as Ganymede, the minion of Jupiter; the Latins, by similar corruption of words, pronounced *Proserpina* for *Persephone, Aesculapius* for *Asclepios, Carthago* for *Carchedo, Pollux* for *Polydeukes, Sybilla* for *Siobulé, masturbare* for *manu stuprare.*

effeminate; if adult or worn out, he is named
exolete. The masculine pleasure (so called
because women allowed themselves much
more rarely to be pedicated than men) is appreciated equally by the active party, the
pedicon, as by the passive party, the patient.
The pleasure of the pedicon is easy to understand, as the enjoyment of the virile member
consists in the intensity of the friction; the
pleasure felt by the patient by the introduction of the member in his entrails is more
difficult to make out,—at least for my feeble
intelligence, for such practices are quite
strange to me. Do not believe, however, that
the pleasure of the patient is only secondary,
nor yet that he prostitutes himself only in
order to do the same afterwards himself, nor
that he remedies in this way the sluggishness
of his own member by the vigorous working
of another man's nerve causing a pleasurable
titillation of the posterior, analogous to that
which Antonius Panormitanus (*Hermaphroditus,* I, 20), tells us may be produced by
inserting the fingers in the anus (19), or still

---

(19) Thus Oenothea, to exicite the lad's feeble nerve,
pushes a leathern mentula (member) into Eucolpius'

better, by beating the same locality with rods, according to Aloysia Sigaea:

"Amongst the men of our acquaintance, I have heard the Marquis Alfonso say that rods act as spurs to the amorous battle; without them he would be sluggish and impotent. He has his buttocks flogged with rods vigorously, his wife being present lying ready on the bed. During the flagellation his tool begins to stiffen, and the more violent the strokes are, the stronger is the tension. When he feels himself in proper condition, he precipitates himself upon his wife, works her with rapid movement, and inundates her with the heavenly gifts of Venus and wins all the delights a man may find in Love" (20) (Dialogue V).

---

anus (Petronius, 138): "Oenothea fetches a leathern contrivance; this she first oiled and sprinkled with pepper and crushed nettle-seeds, and then proceeded to push little by little up my anus." We shall have to speak in chapter VI. of another use of these leathern tools.

(20) According to the author of the *Gynaeology* (German edition, vol. III, p. 392) there are to be found at this day in the London brothels women who make it their business to flagellate customers who desire it.

What else was it but this that so stirred Rousseau, the precocious genius of Geneva, and his boyish member, and brought such ideas into his head, when on one occasion Mlle. Lambercier, cracking the whip upon the buttocks of the child, inflicted that punishment, which he afterwards was longing for all the rest of his life? Hear him relate the circumstance himself in his merry way and with his habitual charm of style, in the first book of the *Confessions;* we only omit small matters, added by the immortal author for the amplification of the narrative:

"As Mlle. Lambercier had for us the affection of a mother, so she had the authority of one, and she carried the latter so far as to inflict upon us the punishment of children when we had deserved it. For a long time she only used threats, and such a threat of a novel punishment seemed very dreadful to me; but after the execution I found the experience less terrible than the expectation, and the oddest thing was, the punishment made me more partial to her, who had inflicted it, than I had been previously. I stood in fact in need of all this affection for her and of all

my natural mildness, in order to hold back
from provoking the same punishment by acting so as to deserve it, for I had found in the
pain, and even in the shame, a mixed feeling,
in which sensuality predominated, and which
left me with more desire than apprehension
of experiencing the same treatment over
again from the same hand. Who would believe that this chastisement of a child eight
years old by the hand of a maiden of thirty
should have influenced my tastes, my longings, my passions for the remainder of my
life? Tormented by I know not what, my
eye feasted ardently upon good-looking
females; they constantly came into my mind
doing to me as Mlle. Lambercier had done.
Imagining only what I had experienced, my
desires did not pass beyond the sort of voluptuous feeling I had known already. In my
foolish fancies, in my erotic fury, in the ex-
travagant acts to which they incited me sometimes, I borrowed in imagination the help of
the other sex, without ever dreaming it was
good for any other use than that which I
wanted to make of it. When in the course of
time I had grown up to manhood, my old taste

of childhood associated itself so much with
the other, that I never could divert the desires
which fired my senses; and this absurdity,
joined to my natural timidity, made me always anything but enterprising with women,
as I dared not say all or could not do all I
wanted; the sort of enjoyment, of which the
other was for me but the last stage, could
neither be initiated by the one who longed
for it, nor guessed by the other who might
have granted it. Thus I have passed through
life coveting, yet not daring to tell the persons
I loved most what it was I coveted. Never
bold enough to declare my inclination, I
amused it as least by ideas in connection with
it. One may judge what such avowals must
have cost me, considering that all through my
life, seized in the presence of those I loved by
the fury of a passion which bereft me of voice,
hearing and sense, and made me tremble all
over convulsively, I never could venture to tell
them my folly, and ask them to add the one
familiarity which I wanted to the other ones.
I only got to it once in my childhood, with another child of my age, and the proposal came
from her."

However to return to our proper subject, from which we have strayed. If pleasure felt by the passive party cannot be conceived to be of a kind, which through the anus is communicated to the mentula (member), we must come to the conclusion that the *patient* experiences in the anus the same kind of irritation which the other party feels in his genital parts; that, therefore, the *patient* feels in that place a real pleasure unknown to those who have not tried it (21). Martial at any rate speaks out without any circumlocution of this rut of the anus:

"Of his anus, split to the naval, not a vestige is left to Carinus; for all that he is in rut to the very navel. Oh! the scurvy lot of the wretch! Bottom he has none,—but he *will* be a cinede" (VI, 37).

An ardour of this strange sort even affected Tullia, as she confesses herself in the pages of Aloysia Sigaea:

"Seeing resistance was in vain, I yielded to

---

(21) In order to appease the ardours of the anus, the Siphnians (Siphnos, one of the Cyclades) were in the habit of introducing a finger up the anus. The Greeks called this proceeding to *siphnianize*. Suidas: *Siphnianize*,—to finger the posterior.

the madmen. Aloysio bends forward over my buttocks, brings his javelin to the back-door, knocks, pushes, finally with a mighty effort bursts in. I gave a groan. Instantly he withdraws his weapon from the wound, plunges it in the vulva and spurts a flood of semen into the wanton furrow of my womb. When all was over, Fabrizio attacks me in the same fashion. With one rapid thrust he introduced his spear, and in less than no time made it disappear in my entrails; for a little time he plays at come and go, and scarce credible as it may sound, I found myself invaded by a prurient fury to such an extent that I have no doubt, that I should get accustomed to it very well, if I chose" (Dialogue VI).

Coelius Rhodiginus confirms this pruriency of the anus in chap. 10. of XV. book of his *Lectiones antiquae.*

"We know", he says, "that the minions experience a very great pleasure in undergoing this shameful act".

And he gives a reason for it, whether good or bad the doctors may decide: "With people whose seminal ducts are not in normal condition, be it that those leading to the mentula are paralysed, as is the case with eunuchs and the like, or for any other reason, the seminal fluid flows back to its source. If this fluid is very abundant with them, it accumulates in great quantities, and then the part where the secretion is accumulated longs for friction. People thus situated like above everything to play the part of *patients*."

Be this as it may, nothing is more certain than the fact of such enjoyment on the part of the *patient*. So highly did the Roman cinedes prize a stiff member between their buttocks, that they could not see a big mentula without their mouths watering; they were ready to give their last penny to enjoy the favours of a man extraordinarily gifted in that way.

Juvenal, IX, v. 32-36:

"Destiny governs man; it influences the parts, which the toga covers. If your star pales, useless will be the length and strength of your member to you,—even though Virro shall have seen you naked with lips that water."

Martial, I, 97:

"He wants to know why I think he is a minion? We bathe together; he never raises his eyes, but gazes with devouring looks at the sodomites; and cannot behold their members without his lips trembling."

And again, II, 51:

"Oftentimes you have no more than a single penny in your box, and that penny more worn than your anus, Hyllus; yet neither baker nor wine shop will have it, but some man who sports an enormous member. Your unfortunate belly must starve for your anus; while the latter devours, the former is famished."

It is therefore not astonishing that the public baths resounded with plaudits, when men with extraordinary members entered them.

Martial, IX, 34:

"If you hear clapping of hands in the bathing hall, Flaccus, you may be sure some deformed person's enormous member is there."

Juvenal, VI, v. 373, 374:

"Far seen, pointed at by all men's fingers, he enters the baths."

It was not without some art that the patients performed their functions. But their business was made up of these two chief requirements:

depilation and knowing how to use the haunches.

Patients took care in the first place to remove the hair carefully from all parts of their body (22); from the lips, arms, chest, legs, the virile parts, and in particular from the altar of passive lust, the anus: Martial, II, 62:

"Pluck out the hair from breast and legs and arms; keep your member cropped and ringed with short hair; all this, we know, you do for your mistress' sake, Labienus. But for whom do you depilate your posteriors?"

And IX, 28:

"While you, Chrestus, appear thus with your parts all hairless, with a mentula like a vulture's neck, and a head as shining as a prostitute's buttocks with never a hair appearing on your leg, and with your pallid lips all shorn

---

((22) Always, however, excepting the head, for they took great care of their head of hair. Horace, Ode X, book IV., says to Ligurinus:

"When those curls are gone, that now descend to your shoulders...".

And (Epode XI, v. 40-43): "Nothing", he says, "will take away his love for Lycisus, save another love for a plump youth, tying up his long hair." In the same sense Martial speaks of *Capillati* (III, 58; II, 57), and of *Comati* (XII, 99).

and bare, you talk of Curius, Camillus, Numa, Ancus, of all the hairy heroes we have ever read of in history, and spout big words and threatenings against theatres and the times. Let but some big-limbed man come into sight, you call him with a nod, and take him off. . . "

And he says, IX, 58:

"Nought is worse worn than Hedylus' rags, save one thing only (he cannot deny it himself), his anus;—this is worse worn than his rags."

In a similar way he has spoken before of the anus of Hyllus as more worn by friction than a poor man's last penny (II, 51), and Suetonius (*Life of Otho,* ch, xii) speaks similarly of the body of Otho, given to the habits of a catamite, and Catullus (Carm. 33) reproaches the younger Vibennius: "You could not sell your hairy buttocks for a doit".

For the same reason Galba requested Icelus to get depilated before he was to take him aside. Suetonius, *Galba,* ch. xxii:

"He was very much given to the intercourse between men, and amongst such he preferred men of ripe age, exolets. It is said that when

Icelus, one of his old bedfellows, came to Spain, to inform him of Nero's death, he, not content with kissing him closely before everyone present, asked him to get at once depilated, and then took him aside with him quite alone."

Moreover even those depilated their anus, who by dint of a rough head of hair and a bristly beard, tried hard to simulate the gravity of the ancient Philosophers. Martial, IX, 48:

"Democritus and Zeno and ambiguous Plato,—all the sages whose portraits we see decked with bristling hair, — you prate of; you might well be Pythagoras' heir and successor; while from your own chin hangs no less imposing a beard. But as bearded man it is a shame for you to receive a rigid member between your smooth posteriors."

Juvenal, II, v. 8-13:

"Put not your trust in faces; everywhere is debauchery rampant! Thou wouldst whip the vicious; Thou! thou!—the most notorious of all Socratic minions! Hair-covered limbs and coarse hair along the arms bespeak a fiery soul; but on your smooth anus the surgeon cuts away the swollen tumours, a grin on his face the while."

Persius, IV, v. 37, 38:

"Tell me, when you comb a scented beard upon your cheeks, why does a shaven member stand forth from your groin?"

This is why Martial (VI, 56) advised Charidemus to get his buttocks depilated, so that he might be taken for a *patient* rather than for a *fellator*:

"Because you thighs bristle with coarse hair, and your chest is shaggy, you think, Charidemus, to leave your words to posterity.

"Take my word, and pluck out the hairs all over your body, and get it certified you depilate your buttocks. What for? you ask. You know they tell many tales about you; make them believe, Charidemus, that you are acting the *patient*."

It was not *patients* only that had themselves depilated; men leading an idle, careless life followed the same practice (23).

---

(23) To depilate one's armpits was, however considered as being necessary to the cleanliness of the body: "One man keeps himself tidy, another neglects himself more than is right; one man depilates his legs, another

"To be depilated, to have the hair dressed in tiers of ringlets, to tipple to excess in the baths,—these practices prevail in the city; still they cannot be said to be customary, for nothing of all this is exempt from blame" (Quintilian, *Instit. orat.*, I, 6).

It is rather surprising that the same Quintilian, whose bile is stirred by curled hair, has let it pass by patiently, that women should bathe together with men:

"If it is a sure sign of adultery for a woman to bathe with men, why! it will be adultery to dine with young friends of the male sex, to have a male friend. You might as reasonably say a depilated body, a languid gait, a womanish robe, are certain signs of effeminacy, of want of virility; for such will seem to many to reveal immorality of character" (*Ibid.*, V, 9).

Martial (II,39) has also noticed, and not once only, the habits of those men who practised feminine arts of the toilette, and looked just as if they had come out of a band-box:

"Rufus, see you that man there on the first

---

does not depilate even his armpits." (Seneca, letter CXIV.)

benches . . . whose oiled curls exhale the whole
shop of Marcelianus, and whose polished arms
shine without a hair to be seen?"

Again, he says, V, 62:

". . . Who is this Crispulus, who has legs
undisfigured by a single hair?"

Even the great Caesar did not disdain this
coquetry, Suetonius, ch. 45:

"He took too much care of his appearance,
to the point of not only having his beard removed with nippers, and shaved with a razor,
but even of being depilated, for which things
he was blamed."

This custom is connected with those Sam-
nite vases, filled with rosin and pitch to be
heated for depilation, and for softening the
pitch, found amongst the properties of Commodus, and which by the orders of Pertinax
were sold by public auction. Julius Capitoli-
nus speaks of them (*Pertinax, 8*). For remov-
ing the hair there were used in fact either
tweezers or an unguent called dropax or psilothrum. Martial mentions the use of tweezers in the Epigram (IX, 28) quoted before;
of dropax or psilothrum he speaks in Book
III, 74:

"You depilate your face with psilothrum and your head with dropax."

And again VI, 93:

"She revives her youth with psilothrum."

And X, 65:

"You rub yourself every day with dropax."

The dropax or psilothrum was obtained by melting rosin in oil (Pliny, *Natural History,* XIV 20):

"Rosin dissolves in oil, and I am ashamed to say, that the most honest use made of this mixture is to serve people as a depilatory."

Aëtius also mentions it in Book III, ch. cxc, of his *Opus Medicum*:

"The simplest dropax is the one called pitchplaster. Dry pitch is diluted with oil; it is applied hot to the skin, which must first be cleanly shaved, under which circumstances it adheres closely. Before the plaster is quite cold, it is taken off, warmed again, and put on afresh; again it is removed before being cold, and this process is repeated several times."

Hence Juvenal's, "Youthfulness by pitch", (VIII, 114), and

"The thighs neglected and dirty with tufts of hair" of Nævolus, to whom he says:

"Your skin has none of the gloss, that of old the well-smeared plaster of hot pitch gave it" (Sat. IX, 13-15).

What else does Martial, mean when (III, 74), he speaks of "Gargilanus' nails,—that cannot be trimmed with pitch?"

Persius (IV, 37-41) has, I presume, joined together both modes of depilation:

"Tell me, when you comb a scented beard upon your cheeks, why does a shaven member stand forth from your groin? Though five strong men weed your plantation and work your parboiled buttocks with the hooked tweezers, I tell you there is no plough will tame that stubborn field!"

Here *forceps* is the same thing as *volsella* (tweezers); while the "parboiled buttocks" would seem to refer to the hot *dropax*. After the application of such a plaster the skin could not but have a boiled look.

Ausonius (*Epigr.* CXXXI.) alludes to this passage of Persius:

"The reason you smooth your groin with hot dropax is that a skin soft and smooth entices the whores, plucked smooth themselves. But that you pluck out the herbage from your parboiled bottom, and polish up with pumice your battered Clazomenae, what means this,— if not that the vice of man with man works in you, and you are a woman behind, a man in front."

The *Clazomenae* are without a doubt the man's buttock, limp and cracked, as those of *patients* will be, as those of Carinus were, whom Martial (XI, 37) blames for "his lacerated anus". Ausonius calls them so from the Greek, in Latin "frango" (I break), thus playing with the name of a city. Gonzalvo the Cordevan makes a similar pun, when, desiring to pedicate, he says, he wishes to go to Aversa; also when he wishes to irrumate the mouth, he says: "I go to the Orient", or when he is about to lick the vulva, in Latin *ligurire*, "I go to Liguria". By calling the Clazomenae hammered (battered) Ausonius means to imply that they were as if polished with a hammer, by having served as an anvil. It is as if my fellow-countrymen were to say in joke of a bald man (in German *Kahl*), "he scratches his polished Kehl". What could be clearer or wittier? Forcellini is therefore wrong in saying this passage of Ausonius has no sense.

Other editors have *inclusas* instead of *incusas*, indicating the fissure which separates the buttocks, by the rotundities of which it is on both sides closed in. But in the first place the Clazomenae may well be the buttocks, they being cleft, though not indeed themselves a cleft; in the second place, who could imagine this miserable man depilated the cleft of the buttocks rather than the buttocks themselves?

Some persons, by a refinement of luxury, employed women to depilate them. Such women called themselves *ustriculae* (from *urere*, to burn), as they made use of a sticky plaster of boiling dropax to burn the hair on the legs and other parts of the body. Tertullian (*De Pallio,* ch. 4), says: "So effeminate as to employ *ustriculae*"; while Salmasius, commenting playfully on the passage, p. 284, declares: Once upon a time *ustriculae* served to depilate the legs; now they serve to harass our minds." Augustus, who according to Suetonius, "was in the habit of singeing his legs with burning nutshells, to make the hair grow more silky" (*Augustus,* ch. 68), no doubt made use of the nimble hands of these *ustriculae*.

Women likewise resorted to depilation

(24), looking upon the fleece of the pubis as something disgusting. Martial:

---

(24) The Greeks did not disdain this strange practice any more than the Romans. Aristophanes, in the *Lysistrata* (v. 89).

"My affair will be tidy with the couchgrass pluck'd off." In the "Frogs" he speaks of dancing girls barely arrived at puberty beginning to tear off the fur" (v. 519); in the *Thesmophoriazusae* again there is mentioned "a *mons Veneris* plucked clean" (v. 719). That the Greeks preferred a bare pubis to a furred one, though we may be of a different opinion, is apparent from another passage of Aristophanes, in the *Lysistrata*, v. 151, 2, where a smooth pubis is represented as a chief incitement to virile ardour:

"If we were to go naked with a smooth pubis, our husband's members would stand, and they would be fain to have us."

As to old women, they likewise denuded their pubis of the bristles in order to appear less decrepit. Martial, X, 90.

"Ligella, do you pluck your old affair, and stir the ashes of your burnt-out fire?

Refinements such as those are for young maidens; you are in error if you think that thing a vulva that a man's member will no longer recognize".

The depilation of the vulva was also used as a punishment.

Aristophanes, *Tesmophoriazusae*, 545, 6.

"We will pluck her pubis, and teach her so, woman as she is, not to speak ill of women."

The same punishment was inflicted upon adulterous women taken in the act; a black radish or a mullet was introduced into her anus, which was then depilated, as

".... Nor yet one of your mother's pots full of foul rosin, such as the women of the outer suburbs use to depilate themselves withal" (XII, 32).

As men employed women to free them of hair, so women offered their pubis without shame to men for the same office. Pliny's bile rises at this (*Nat. Hist.*, XXIX, 8) : "Women are not afraid to show their pubis. It is but too true, nothing corrupts manners more than the art of the medical man."

The emperors themselves condescended to undertake this office for their concubines.

Sutonius, *Domitian,* ch. 22:

"It was rumoured, that he was fond of depilating his concubines himself, and would bathe amid a crowd of the most infamous courtezans."

Lampridius, *Heliogabalus,* chap. 31:

"In his baths he was always together with the women, and he made their toilets with psilothrum: he used psilothrum likewise for his beard, and, disgusting to relate, the same which the women had just been using. With

well as her pubis, with burning cinders. Aristophanes, *Clouds,* 1079:

his own hand he shaved off the fleece from the virile part of his pedicons, and then shaved his own beard."

What Lampridius finds so repugnant, is that the emperor did not hesitate to use upon his beard the same ointment, which the women had just been applying as a plaster upon the pubis, and which he used at once and before the bad smell had evaporated.

But to return to our *patients,* they also were not in want of illustrious lovers, who took care to depilate them; an example of this we find in the emperor Hadrian, according to Spartianus, who says, ch. 4:

"That he corrupted the freedmen of Trajan, made the toilet of his minions, and often depilated them, while he was attached to the Court, is generally believed."

In what other way can we believe Hadrian to have made the toilet of these minions, if not in the same way in which Heliogabalus made

---

"What, must you suffer the empalement with the radish, and the hot cinders?"

Suetonius, under the word ——————: "Thus they treated adulteresses who had been caught in the act: they took black radishes and planted them in their anus, which they rubbed with hot cinders, after having torn out the hair."

the toilet of his females, with psilothrum, particularly as it is added that he depilated them frequently? We may take it for granted that he used that ointment, or that he rubbed their faces with moistened bread, either to improve their skin or to hinder the beard growing too soon. Suetonius, *Otho,* ch. 12:

"He shaved his face every day, and rubbed it with damp bread, a habit which he had contracted when the first down began to appear, so as not to get bearded."

Juvenal (II,107), has aimed an arrow of the same sort at Otho:

"It surely is the duty of a mighty Captain .... to keep his skin right smooth .... and knead bread with his fingers to make a plaster for his face."

What wonder then if the women cherished similar artifices? Who can help thinking of the woman depicted with such marvellous art by Juvenal, from verse 460 to verse 472 of that Sixth Satire, to which Salmasius gave the epithet, of "divine"? "Her face is all puffy with bread crumbs, where the lips of the poor husband keep sticking", to such an extent, that one doubts:

". . . . Whether her countenance, plastered
and *massaged* with so many preparations,
overlaid with poultices of boiled and moistened flour, should be called a face at all,—or a
sore. . . At last she peels her face, removes the
outermost layers. For the first time she may
be recognizd for herself. Then she treats her
skin with asses' milk, for which she drags
about in her train a herd of asses,—and would
take them with her, if she were exiled to the
North Pole."

For painting the face it seems that a coat-
ing of chalk was used, as in the case of the
Pederast mentioned in Petronius, who per-
spired so violently in working vainly the groin
of Eucolpus:

"From his perspiring forehead flowed rivulets of acacia juice, and in the wrinkles of his
cheeks there was such a mass of chalk that you
might have believed you saw a wall exposed
to the wind and washed by the rain" (*Satyri-
con,* ch. 23).

But let us leave all these nasty preparations,
before we find ourselves stuck fast in them.

We have said that another branch of this
business, on the part of the *patient,* consists in

cevere. A *patient cevet,* who during the action wriggles and moves his haunches up and down, so as to enjoy more pleasure himself and give more pleasure to the pedicon. Women, doing the same in copulation, are said to *crissare.* Martial, III, 95:

"Nay! you pedicate finely, Naevolus; you ply your haunches right well."

Juvenal, II, 20-23:

". . . Virtue on their lips, they ply their buttocks.—'Shall I honour you, in the act of your back-play, Sextus?' says the infamous Varillus . . ."

The same author, IX, 40:

"With calculated art moves his haunches."

Plautus, in the *Pseudolus,* III, 75:

"Soon as ever the fellow cowers down, ply your haunches in time to him."

For this reason some authorities hold, I do not know whether rightly or wrongly, the word *cinede* to come from the fact that the wretches known by that name are in the habit of *wriggling the private parts.* Undoubtedly the suppleness of the thighs, the agility of the buttocks are counted almongst the particular talents of cinedes in Petronius, ch. 23:

Enter a Cinede reciting these verses:

"Hither, come hither, cinede wantons,—stretch the foot and take your course, fly with soles in the air, with supple thighs, and nimble buttocks, and libertine hands, — all ye old, emasculated minions of Delos, come!"

To this subject also refers Epig. XXXVI of the Ist Book of the *Hermaphroditus,* edited by us; which consult, reader, if worth your while. As he who wriggles with his haunches does it to please somebody, people use the word *cevere* also to convey the meaning of sycophancy or adulation. Thus: "An, Romule, ceves" (What Romulus, you fawn too?) in Persius (I, 87); in the same way *irrumate* is used in the sense of an outrage, affront.

That women *can* be pedicated, exactly the same as men, is indicated by nature; that they *have* consented, is proved by numerous testimonies in Antiquity. — Apuleius, *Metamorphoses,* III, p. 138:

"While we were thus prattling, a mutual desire invaded our minds and roused our limbs; having undressed entirely we gave ourselves up to the transports of Venus. I soon

felt tired. Fotis of her own good will offered
me the catamite corollary."

Martial, IX, 68:

"All night long I possessed a lewd young
maiden, whose complaisant demeanor it were
impossible to excel. Exhausted with a thousand modes of love. I asked for the puerile
service, which she granted at once before I
had finished my asking."

The same, XI, 105, reproaches his wife as
follows:

"You refuse to pedicate; yet Cornelia al-
lowed it to Gracchus, Julia to Pompey, and
Portia did it for Brutus. Ere the Derdanian
Cupbearer served the wine, Juno herself acted
Ganymede for Jupiter."

Tullia permitted the same to Aloysio and
Fabrizio, in Aloysia Sigaea; we have quoted
the passage. Crispa tastes the same variety of
pleasure, in Epigram LXXI of Ausonius:

"She lets herself be done in either orifice."

The ancient Greeks took great delight in
the posterior Venus. One can scarcely express
what fervent admirers they were of beautiful
buttocks; it went so far, that young girls competed in public, before an assemblage sitting

as it were in another "Judgment of Paris" to pronounce which of them was the most gifted in that respect. Athenaeus (XII, 80) informs us that in the environs of Syracuse a villager had two daughters who often quarrelled as to which of them had the finest posteriors; one day they showed them on the highway to a young man from Syracuse, who chanced to be passing, and asked him to adjudicate between them. He decided in favour of the elder sister, fell at once violently in love with her, and on his return home he told his younger brother what had befallen him. The latter went forthwith to see the two girls, and became enamoured of the younger. Soon they got married to the two youths, who were opulent, and they were called by their fellow-citizens the *Callipygi,* because, although of lowly birth, their posteriors served them for a dowry. Full of gratitude, they dedicated a temple to Venus, under the title of Venus Callipygos (Venus of the beauteous buttocks).

It will not surprise you, that any young girl remarkable for her beautiful posteriors amongst her companions was all the more in request for the puerile office, and all the more

disposed to lend herself to it. Mania consented to it in favour of Demetrius, as testified by
Machon, in Athenaeus (XIII, 42), when the
king wanting to enjoy her buttocks, she ac-
cepts his gift, and says:

"Son of Agamemnon, it is now *your* turn to
have them (25)."

A certain young man, Ponticus by name,
exacted the same corollary in the morning
from Gnathena, whom he had possessed all
night; it is again Machon who tells us the
story (*ibid.*, XIII, 43). Demophon, the minion of Sophocles, asked the same favour of
Nico (26) who being famed for the beauty of

---

(25) To understand this, the sentence must be complete; the worthy Forberg takes his readers far too
learned; Mania, in the poem of Machon, says to Demetrius, offering her buttoks:
"Son of Agamemnon, it is now *your* turn to have
them,—you who have ever been so liberal with your
own." (Note of the translator.)

(26) The following is the passage from Machon, as
quoted by Athenaeus; without a knowledge of it Forberg's allusion remains obscure:
"...Demophon, Sophocles' minion, when still a youth
had Nico, already old and surnamed the she-goat; they
say she had very fine buttocks. One day, he begged of
her to lend them to him. 'Very well,' she said with a
smile,—'Take from me, dear, what you give to Sophocles.'" (Note of the translator.)

her buttocks,—"she is said to have had an exceedingly beautiful bottom"—was afraid he might lend them to Sophocles (*ibid.,* XII, 45). Gnathaenion (*ibid.,* XIII, 44) made an ingenious excuse for having been similarly complaisant. A certain tinker having ungenerously boasted he had five times running mounted that little courtezan in that way, Andronicus, whom she preferred to everybody else, got to hear it, and reproached her bitterly for having allowed such a blackguard to enjoy her so abundantly in a posture which his prayers never obtained from her. Gnathaenion replied that, not caring to have her breasts handled by a fellow black with dirt and soot, it had appeared to her better to take that posture, so as to receive the least possible fraction of the wretched creature's body. Plate XXVII of the *Monuments du culte secret des dames romaines* presents the picture of a man pedicating a woman.

It is, however, not without some inconvenience, or even danger, that one lends oneself to the passive part. Aloysia Sigaea, Past-Mistress in the Sciences of Love, enlightens us on this point:

"In the first place intolerable sufferings are inflicted upon the *patient,* for in most cases he is invaded by too large a stake; hence frightful infirmities, incurable by all the art of Aesculapius. The confining muscles are ruptured, and consequently the excrements cannot be held back and escape. What could be more disgusting? I have known noble ladies afflicted with cruel maladies to such a degree by eruptions and ulcers, that it took them two or three years to recover their health. I myself (Tullia) have not escaped scot free from the accursed embraces of Aloysio and Fabrizio. When they first forced their darts in, I endured atrocious pain, but soon the feeling of slight titillation consoled me... When however I reached home again, I felt a burning pain at the place they had lacerated: I felt myself consumed by an itching as if I were on fire, and in spite of the nursing of Donna Orsini, it cost much trouble to extinguish that confounded fire. If my lacerations had been neglected, I should have died a miserable death" (Dial. VI).

You understand now why the young slave of Naevolus (Martial III, 71) had pain at the anus; why the same Martial (VI, 37) says Carinus' posteriors had to be cut; and where the sting lies in the following distich:

"You, who know all the reasons and weighty arguments of the sects, — come tell me, what dogma is it bids you be perforated" (IX, 48).

This effeminate philosopher, who affected to speak as though he had been the successor and heir of Pythagoras, was indeed bound, if anyone was, to know the reasons of lacerations (27) of the anus, and the weights of men's members. He was accustomed to the passive part, of whom Ausonius says in mockery, as we saw a little above, that his *clazomenae* served as an anvil:

Men preferred to be supposed *pedicators* rather than *patients;* hence Martial's witty epigram:

"It is now many a long day, Lupus, that Charisianus has been saying he cannot pedicate. But whenever his friends asked him why, he said his bowels were relaxed" (XI, 89).

---

(27) *Secta,* sect (from *sequor*) may also be derived from *secare,* to cut, and thus mean: laceration. (Note of the translator.)

Would you see the picture of a man engaged in pedication? he is being interrupted in the midst of his business, but the drawing is not the less pleasant for that. The engraving belonging to chapter III. of the third part of *Felicia,* presents this position.

Who does not know that the Greeks and Roman were intrepid pedicons and determined cinedes? In the Greek and Latin authors, to the indignation of the pedagogues, the male Venus parades on every page:

"All burnt with the same fire"— we are quoting Aloysia Sigaea, and we could not express ourselves better or more elegantly. We are, however, going to make annotation to this extract,—"all burnt with the same fire, the common people, the higher classes, the King. This depravity cost Philip, King of Macedon, his life (28) ; he died by the hand

---

(28) Justinus tells the tale somewhat differently: "Pausanias had had to undergo since his puberty the violence of Attalus, who added to this indignity a crying outrage: having invited him to a feast and made him drunk, he not only satisfied upon him, when full of wine, his brutal lust, but allowed him to be used by all the guests like a vile courtezan, and made him the laughing stock of his equals. Unable to bear this infamy, Pausanias carried his complaint before Philip many and many a

of Pausanias, whom he had outraged. It sub-
jected Julius Caesar to the passion of King
Nicomedes (29),—Caesar, "wife of all men,
and husband of all women" (30).

---

time, but the King always put him off with illusory
promises. When Pausanias however saw Attalus elevated to the rank of the Chief of the Army, his fury
turned against Philip, and the vengeance which he
could not take upon his enemy, he took upon the iniquit-
ous judge." (IX, 6).

(29) Suetonius, *Julius Caesar,* ch. 48: "Not content
with having written in some of his letters that Cæsar
was conducted by the guards to the bed-chamber of the
King, slept there in a golden bed hung with purple, and
that he allowed the bloom of his youth to be blighted
in Bithynia, Cicero said to him one day in the midst of
the Senate, where Cæsar was defending the case of Nysa,
the daughter of King Nicomedes, and spoke of his obli-
gations to that King: Pray, let us pass over all this; it
is only too well known what you have received, and what
you have given."

On the day of his triumph over the Gauls, the soldiers
sung the following verses, amongst those which are
usually sung behind the triumphal car, and they are well
known.

"Cæsar has subdued the Gauls, and Nicomedes Cæsar: this day is Cæsar triumphant for having subdued
the Gauls, and Nicomedes, who subdued Cæsar, has no
triumph."

Catullus (*carm.* 57):

"How well they go together, those shameless cinedes,
Mamurra the *patient,* and Cæsar."

(30) Suetonius, *Julius Cæsar,* ch. 51: Nor yet did he
respect the conjugal bed in the provinces; this appears

Augustus did not escape this shame (31), Tiberius (32) and Nero gloried in it. Nero

from the distich, also sung by the soldiers at the triumphal entry:

"Citizens mind your wives; we bring you the bald-headed adulterer. You expended gold in Gaul; here you are taking your change."

The same author (*Julius Cæsar,* ch. 52) says: "Helvius Cinna, tribune of the people, admitted to many people, that he had drawn up and kept ready a law by the instructions of Cæsar, to bring it forward during his absence, by which he would be at liberty, with a view to leaving offspring, to marry whom he would and as many wives as he wished. So that nobody should be in any doubt about the notoriety of his lewdness and infamy, Curio, the elder, in one of his pleadings, calls him the husband of all women, and the wife of all husbands."

(31) "Sextus Pompeius reproached him for being effeminate, and Marc Anthony says he bought his adoption from his uncle (or rather his great-uncle) by prostituting himself to him. On a day of public games all the world understood and applied to him very demonstratively the following verses, spoken of a Priest of Cybelé, Mother of the Gods, playing the tambourine":

"See you how a cinede governs the world with a finger?" (Suetonius, *Augustus,* ch. 68.)

A picture representing Augustus playing the part of a *patient,* is in the *Monuments de la vie privée des douze Césars,* pl. VI., and another of Cæsar and Nicomedes, pl. I.

(32) "It is even said, that during a sacrifice, he could not restrain himself, smitten with the pretty face of the incense-bearer; the divine service barely finished, he took the youth aside, and debauched him, and then did as

married Tigellinus (33), and was himself
espoused by Sporus (34). Trajan (35), the

much for his brother, who played the flute. Soon afterwards he ordered their legs to be broken, because they
reproached each other with their infamy (Suetonius,
Tiberius, ch. 44). The act of this madman is represented on pl. XX. in the work of d'Hancarville, cited on
a previous page.

(33) And also Pythagoras. "One would have thought
that nothing was left for him in the way of debauchery,
and that he had reached the limits of depravity, if he
had not a few days later chosen out of this infamous
herd a certain Pythogoras, whom he took for his husband with all the solemnity of a marriage. The *flammeum* was put on the Emperor's head, the auspices were
consulted, neither dowry nor nuptial torches were forgotten; all was done openly, even those things, which, if
done with a woman, are hidden by the night (Tacitus,
Annals, XV, 37). The man called Pythagoras by Tacitus, appears to be the same to whom Suetonius (*Nero,*
ch. 29), gives the name of Doryphorus, either on account
of his services, or by mistake. "He took for husband the
freedman Doryphorus in the same way in which Sporus
had taken him himself for husband, and he counter-
feited the cries and sobbings of virgins when losing their
maidenhead." Plate XXXVIII of the above quoted
work shows an illustration of this anecdote.

(34) "He went so far as to try to change a young man
into a woman; his name was Sporus, and he had him
castrated; having given him a dowry, he caused him to
be brought to him with the *flammeum* on his head, and
married him with all the nuptial solemnities. There has
come down to us an appropriate saying on somebody's
part, namely, whether it might not have been better
for human kind if Domitian, his father, had married a

best of rulers, was accompanied by a *paeda-gogium,* while he marched from victory through the Orient. What he named his *pae-gogium,* while he marched from victory to victory through the Orient. What he named his *paedagogium* was a troop of pretty lads, well developed, whom he called day and night to come to his arms. Antinous served as mistress to Hadrian,—a rival to Plotina, but more fortunate than she was (36). The em-

---

woman of that sort. He made Sporus dress himself in the costume of the Empresses, and had him carried in his litter; he travelled with him in that way, taking him through the meetings and markets in Greece, and soon after in Rome, about the time of the Sigillarian festiv-ities, kissing him from time to time" (Suetonius, *Nero,* chap. 28). Plate XXXIV in the repeatedly quoted French work, gives a representation of the abominable wedding.

(35) "He (Hadrian) enjoyed the affection of Trajan, but this did not save him from the malevolence of the pedagogues of the young boys Trajan loved so ardently" (Spartianus, *Hadrian,* ch. 2).

(36) "He lost, during his navigation of the Nile, his dear Antinous, and wept for him like a woman. There are sundry allegations about this Antinous; some say he was devoted to Hadrian, others point to the beauty of his shape, and to the pleasure Hadrian experienced with him. At the instance of Hadrian the Greeks placed him in the ranks of the Gods, and affirmed that he gave oracular decisions; those oracles, it is said, were com-posed by Hadrian himself" (Spartianus, *Hadrian,* ch.

peror mourned over his death, and placing
the dead man amongst the Gods, he raised altars and temples in his honour. Antonius
Heliogabalus, nephew of Severus, was accustomed, an old author says (37), to have pleas-

---

14). St. Jerome says in the *Hegesippus*: "Antinous, a
slave of the Emperor Hadrian, after whom a circus was
named the Antinoian, founded also a town bearing his
name (Antinoia), and established an Oracle in the
temple."

(37) "Who, indeed, could put up with a ruler who
imbibed pleasure through all the cavities in his body?
Not even a beast would be suffered to do so. At Rome
his only care was to send out emissaries, who had to look
out for and to bring to the court the best shaped men for
his enjoyment. He had a performance of the comedy of
"Paris" in his palace, played the part of Venus himself,
and suddenly dropping his clothes, he appeared naked
with one hand on his chest and the other covering his
pudenda; he then knelt down and offered his raised
buttocks to his pedicon" (Lampridius, *Heliogabalus,* ch.
5). And a little farther on: "He loved Hierocles to such
a degree as to kiss his virile parts, a thing I blush to report; he said that he thus celebrated the Floralia" (*Ibid.,*
ch. 6). He did not hesitate to repeat the infamous wedding of Nero with Pythagoras: "Zoticus had such a
power over him that the principal officials of the state
treated him as though he really were the husband of the
Emperor. He married him, and made him consummate
the marriage in the presence of the giver away of the
bride, telling him, "Push in, Magira!" And this was
done at a time when Zoticus was ill" (Lampridius, ch.
10). Zoticus was called Magira on account of the profes-
sion of his father, who had been a cook.

ures administered to him through all the orifices in his body; his contemporaries looked upon him as a monster. Before this Venus grave philosophers danced in company with pederasts. Alcibiades and Phaedo slept with Socrates (38), when they wanted to get their tutor into good humour. It is from this kind of amours practised by the venerable man, that is derived the erotic phrase: to love *Socratically*. Every action and every word of

---

(38) Socrates, as is well known, has not been in want of warm defenders; Brucker (*Critical History of Philosophy*, I, pp. 539, 540), may stand for all of them. Undoubtedly Plato, in *Symposium*, brought in Alcibiades, who says he recollects, to use the expression of Cornelius Nepos (*Alcibiades*, ch. 2.) "to have passed a night with Socrates, but not otherwise than a son might with his father." But Xantippe, and it is not surprising, was indignant that her husband should be on such familiar terms with a good-looking youth like Alcibiades; and Aelian (*Varide Historiae*, XI, 12), relates that she stamped upon a cake sent by Alcibiades, which made Socrates laugh and cry out: "What are you doing? You cannot eat it now. I do not care for it at all!" But, Socrates! good morals and such friends are incompatible. Enough to name amongst the disciples of Socrates Plato, whom Diogenes Laërtius (III, 23), declares to have loved Aster, Phaedrus, Alexis, and before all Dion; he quotes an epigram of Plato on Dion, ending thus:

"O you, who have so fiercely burnt my heart with love, you Dion!"

Socrates were held as sacred by all sects of philosophers; they built a temple and erected an altar in his honour; all his actions had legal force, and his words the authority of an oracle. The philosophers did not turn away from the example set by their Hero (for Socrates took rank with the Heroes) and new national divinity. Lycurgus, the Spartan legislator, living some centuries before Socrates, refused the title of a good and deserving citizen to any man who had not a friend that served him as a concubine. He willed it that virgins should perform naked on the stage, so that the view of their charms freely exposed, should dull in men that sensual longing which by the aid of nature draws them to women, that they might thus reserve all their passion for their friends and companions. For what men see every day loses half its effect.

Again, why speak of the Poets (39)? Ana-

---

(39) Valerius Maximus (IX, 12) relates of Pindar: "One day, at the Gymnasium, Pindar, leaning his head against the breast of a young lad, whom he loved above all (Suidas says his name was Theoxenes), fell asleep; no sooner had the head of the establishment seen him asleep than he ordered all the doors to be closed, for fear

creon (40), was hotly in love with Bathyllus; almost all pleasantries of Plautus have this subject for their aim; they are of this kind:

"I shall do like the lads, I will cower down over a hamper (41)."

---

of the poet being awakened." Athenaeus on his part (XIII, 81) tells us of Sophocles: "Sophocles loved boys to the same degree as Euripides loved women"; and a little farther on (ch. 82) he relates the story of a youth whom Sophocles enjoyed, but at the price of his mantle, which the rogue abstracted. Euripides, having been informed of this adventure, mocked the poet for having been thus done: "I also", he said, "have had him, but he got nothing else out of me." I am surprised that this passage of Athenaeus should have appeared doubtful to the celebrated Casaubon, on account of the expression "got out of me" which is quite correct and applicable. Sophocles and Euripides had both lavished their white fluids upon the little rogue; but from one of them he got besides a mantle, from the other nothing else.

(40) "No less fiercely burned the love of Anacreon of Teos, they say, for the Samian youth Bathyllus" (Horace, *Epodes,* XIV, 9, 10).

(41) The actual words of Plautus are:
"I must do the puerile service: I will cower down over a hamper" (*Cistellaria* IV, sc. I, v. 5),—which means, I will bend down to the hamper, raising the buttocks, and thus present them to the pedicon. This is, in fact, what is called, the "puerile office", and which Apuleius (*Metam.* III, ch. 2), calls "the puerile corollary". Martial (IX, 68) says simply, *"illud puerile."* *Conquinescere* is according to Nonius, p. 531, Gottfried's edition, to curve the spine, an expression designat-

ing in particular the passive posture as we have seen in the *Pseudolus*:

"When he curves the spine, then simultaneously wriggle your buttocks."

Some authors have also used a still more forcible expression, *"Ocquinescere,"* vis., "to cower low down" (Nonius, p. 567). Pomponius, on word *"Prostibulum"*: "I have never forced pedication upon any citizen; I have always abstained, unless the patient had asked me and cowered down of his own free will." And on word *"Pistor"*: "Unless somebody anticipated my desires, willingly crouching down so that I could do the thing securely." This position of the patient cowering down is very rarely alluded to; the question generally turns upon his kneeling. "Thus," says Lampridus of Heliogabalus, he offered himself with the buttocks raised to the pedicon" (ch. 5). Heliogabalus was kneeling, and not crouching. The same is the case with Timarchus in Lucian: "All that were near you remember it; they have seen you on your knees, while your accomplice did you know what" (*Apophras,* p. 152, vol. VII.—Works of Lucian edit. by J.-P. Schmid). If you would like to see these two postures, you will find them in the *Monuments de la vie privée des douze Césars,* pl. XXVII., a *patient* crouching, and pl. XXXVIII, a *patient* kneeling.

From the fact that men wanting to void their excrement when out of doors cower down, it has come about that **passive pederasts were said to sh...t,**—in fact to sh...t the active party's member as it goes in and out of the anus. Hence in the *priapeia,* LXX:

"Look at me, thief, and realize the weight of the member you will have to sh...t." Martial (IX, 70) also plays on the word:

"When you love a woman, Polycharmus, you always sh...t before you have done. Tell me, Polycharmus, what you do, when you pedicate?"

Or again:

"The soldier's poniard did it fit your sheath (42)?"

That grand master of the art of poetry, Maro, who won the surname of Parthenias by his ingenuousness and innate modesty, cherished a certain Alexander, whom Pollio had given to him as a present, and he has celebrated him under the name of Alexis (43). Ovid suffered from the same malady; he however preferred young girls to lads, because in his amusement he wanted reciprocal pleasure, and not a selfish enjoyment. He said he loved the pleasure "of the simultaneous ejaculation of both parties" (44), and for this reason he was less given to the love of boys.

Young girls and wives finding themeslves

---

(42) *Pseudolus,* IV, sc. VII, 85.

(43) You might very well, Aloysia, have quoted Horace too (*Epodes,* XI):

"'Now Lyciscus holds me in love-bonds, from which neither friendly advice, nor humiliating affronts avail to liberate me.

And *Satires,* I, ii, v. 116-119.

"When your privates are swelling, if some maid-servant or slave-boy is at hand for you to assail forthwith, do you choose rather to burst with desire? Nay! not I!"

(44) Art of Love, II, 683, 684.

neglected, the first by those they loved, the
other ones by their husbands, instead of offering their services only as females, resolved
to play the part of the lads. The depravity
became so great that this complaisance was
actually extorted from brides, as it was before from married women; in fact the husband went at the young wife pederastically,
and the two sexes were joined in one and the
same body. In the facetious poems of the ancients, Priapus (45) threatens every thief of
vegetables from his garden that comes near
his weapon, to make him sacrifice what in the
first night the bride accords to her ardent
husband, for fear that he may wound another
part.

Making use of his imagination with the
licence ever granted both to painters and
poets, Valerius Martial (46) pretends to

---

(45) Priapeia, II.

(46) Epigr. 44, book IX:

"Catching me with a boy, you harass me with your
cries, and you tell me, my wife, that you have posteriors
too.

Many and many a time did Juno say the same to Jupiter the Thunderer; yet he continued to sleep with
slender Ganymede.

He of Tyrius, laying his bow aside, bent Hylas under

hear his wife grumble that she also had buttocks, and that he had no need of boys. "Juno", she says, "also pleased Jupiter from that side." Tho poet is not to be convinced, he answers her that the part taken by a boy is one thing, and that of the wife another, and that she ought to be satisfied with hers.

---

him; think you therefore that Megara was without buttocks? Dephné, by her flight, vexed Phœbus, but his love's ardour found relief in the end in the boy Oebalius. Although Briseis slept, often with her backs turned upon him, his smooth-skinned friend Patroclus was more to the taste of the son of Aeacus.

Cease then, wife, to call your affairs by masculine names; better consider you have two vulvas.

His Epigram XII, 98, treats of the same matter:

Knowing as you do the honest walk and fidelity of your husband, and that he never misuses your bed with concubines, why, foolish woman, torment yourself about those venal boy lovers,—brief and fugitive is the pleasure from their complaisance!

They are more useful to you than to their master, I tell you, for they make him think that one wife is better than they all. They give what you will not give;—But I will, you say, so that the volatile husband stray not from the conjugal bed.

But it is not the same thing, I want a fig not an orange, and you must know theirs is a fig, yours an orange; Look! a matron, a woman like you, must know what belongs to her. Leave to boys what is theirs, and do you make the best of what is yours."

Under the name-boards (47) and the lamps
(48) in the brothels sat (49) boys as well as
girls, the first dressed in the feminine stola,
the latter in the manly tunic, and with their
hair dressed like boys. Under the guise of
one sex was found the other. Asia (50) was

(47) Some prostitutes sat (Plautus, *Poenulus,* I., ii.,
v. 54), others stood: "Another man will only have the
harlot that stands upright in the unclean brothel,"
(Horace, Sat. I, ii., v. 30.)

(48) Juvenal's Messalina (VI., v. 123) prostitutes
herself "under the fictitious name - board of Lycisca."
Petronius: "I see men gliding in stealthily between the
name-boards and the naked prostitutes; I understood,
alas, too late, that I had been introduced into a bad place.
(*Satyr.* ch. 7.) Martial (XI., 46):
"When you pass the threshold of a chamber with
name-board over the door, whether it be a boy or a girl
that greeted you with a smile".....
That the prostitutes changed their names is apparent
from a passage in Plautus (*Poenulus,* V, iii, 20, 21:
"For to-day they were to change their names, and
will lend their bodies for infamous traffic."

(49) Horce, Sat. II, vii, 48, 49:
".....Every woman that naked beneath the bright
lamplight endured the thrusts of a swollen member."
Juvenal, VI, 130, 131.
"Foul with the reek of the lamp, she bore to the Im-
perial couch the stink of the brothel."

(50) Authors vary on this point. Herodotus: "The
Persians pollute young boys; they have learned it from
the Greeks (I, 135). Plutarch refutes the assertion:
"How can the Persians be indebted to the Greeks for

the original home of this pest, then Africa got
infected, and soon the scourge invaded Greece
and the adjoining countries of Europe (51).
In Thrace Orpheus was the importer and
supporter of this unclean pleasure. The Thra-
cian women, finding themselves held in contempt, ...

"During the sacred feasts and the noctur-
nal orgies of Bacchus, tore the youth to pieces,

---

these impurities, when all historians are agreed upon
the fact that they had eunuchs before they had ever come
near to the Grecian seas?" (Of the Maliciousness of
Herodotus, p. 857, vol. II of Frankfort edition of 1620).
Athenaeus: "Pederastia was first introduced in Greece
by the Cretans, as is related by Timaeus; other authors
however have asserted that the man who first imported
that sort of love was Laius, who, having been hospitably
received by Pelops, fell in love with Chrysippus, the son
of his host, carried him off in his chariot, and fled to
Thebes." (XIII, 79.) And who has not heard of the
incontinence of the inhabitants of Sodom?

(51)   Particularly in Euboea, whence the expression,
"Chalcidize", meaning, according to Hesychius, to pedicate, because masculine loves flourished among the
Chalcidians. "Phicidize" is another expression for the
same thing from the name of a town now unknown;
Suidas: "Phicidize, to be a Pederast", and similarly,
"Siphnianize" from Siphnos, an island in the Ægean;
Hesychius says: "Sipnianize, that is to finger the anus;
the inhabitants of Siphnos are, in fact, given to the
practice of pederastia." We have seen above that the
meaning of Siphnianize has been perverted.

and bestrewed the wide plains with his limbs. (Virgil, *Georg.* IV, 521, 522.)

It is alleged that in those ancient times the Celts (52) ridiculed those amongst them who kept aloof from this practice; such could expect neither civil employment nor honours. Those, that preserved the purity of their morals were shunned as impure. "In a town where everyone is mad, it is not good to be alone sane, and by reason of its not being good it is not advisable." (Dialogue VI.)

This ends our brilliant extract from Aloysia Sigaea.

Even in our own days (53) the taste for the

---

(52) Athenaeus, XIII, 79: "Of all the barbarians the Celts, although their women are most beautiful—it is, therefore, not surprising that an ardent amateur of "fine women," such as Julius Caesar is described to us, should in the Gallic Provinces have been not over respectful to the conjugal bed—the Celts take more pleasure in pederastia than any other Nation, to such a degree that amongst them it is no rarity to find a man lying between two minions.

(53) Pardon me, illustrious Marcus Pullarius, for having almost forgotten you. Ausonius, Epigr. LXX.:

"Which Marcus? The one they call the "cat that catches boys", he who tarnishes all the purity of childhood, who plies with his back-door tool the rearward Venus, the poet Lucilius' *subulo,* his *pullipremo."*

Ausonius calls him the pullarian cat, because he hun-

male Venus has not disappeared, witness the
Persians, who are very much addicted to this
kind of pleasure, as is related by those who
have travelled in their country. Amongst
others there is Adam Lhuilier, chapter 15,
book V, of his *Itinerary*. If we may trust to
Aloysia Sigaea, the Italians and Spaniards
did it; also the Dutchmen, with whom towards the middle of the XVIIIth. Century,
as J. David Michaëlides tells us in his *Treatise on the Law of Moses* (in Dutch), §258,
this habit was so much in vogue, that the punishment of death was hardly of avail against
it; also the Parisians, according to the Author
of the *Gynaeology* (in German, vol. II, p.
427), a fully competent authority, who adds
that in almsot all the great cities of Europe
there are to be found plenty of people who,
either being satiated with the ordinary pleasure, or afraid of infectious diseases, prefer the

---

ted after young lads (puelli) as the cat gives chase to
birds; he calls him, applying to him the same epithets as
"Lucilius, who Satires he had the opportunity of reading,—more fortunate in this than we,—a *subulo* (from
subula, an awl), wanting to make it understood that
with his member he transfixed, like a cobbler with his
awl, the anus of cinedes; and *pullipremo,* from his compressing in his work young lads.

posterior to the anterior Venus,—the English
always excepted, who abominate this practice. Not to be for ever talking generalities
and never giving definite instances, the cases
of Gonzalvo of Cordova (54) and of Ven-
dôme (55), both of them excellent Generals,
have been made notorious enough by histori-
cal documents; to these we could add other
still more illustrious examples, taken from
our own time and made known by a heedless
fame; that of a great author, of a great king,
the father of his country, and of a man, who
during his life gained general admiration by
the penetration of his intellect, and the splen-
dour of his language, and whose knowledge

---

(54) "Menacing with his couched lance some youth
(he was a determined pedicon), he would say he intended to go to Aversa, a famous town" (Aloysia Sigaea,
Dialogue VII).

(55) See the "History of the Eighteenth Century",
by Christ. Dan. Voss (in German, Part V, p. 364). As
to pedicons of less exalted position, of whom mention is
made by the widow of Philip, first Duke of Orleans, in
her amusing letters, pp. 74, 284, 350), which appeared
about thirty years ago, there are: the Cardinal de Bouil-
lon, the Chevalier de Lorraine, the Comte de Marsan,
Francois Louis, Prince de Conti. These together with
the Comte de Varmandois, a cinede this last, must rest
content to appear in a mere foot-note.

embraces all branches of knowledge, not only the ordinary ones, but the profoundest and most abstruse (56),—a man that might well propose the riddle of the Sphinx to his eminent confrère in whom we delight to admire the power of a truly Ciceronian eloquence, unknown in Germany since the death of the great Ernesti. These examples, I say, we could easily allege, were we not apprehensive of raising, quite contrary to our purpose and intention, a feeling of odium against the pious memory of most distinguished men.

Do you wish for any more? Pacificus Maximus offers a goodly number, both of the active and the passive parties. *Elegy* I, p. 107, of the Paris edition:

"The sole cause of my badness was my master,—the man my father and mother incautiously entrusted me to. He was the king of pedicons; not one escaped his lust, so artful and winning was he. Many a thing I learned, I had better have left unknown; much did I absorb through my rectum, much through my lips."

---

(56) Do not misunderstand what I say. It is not for an honest man to sharpen his wits at the expense of another's book.

Elegy II, to Ptolemy (p. 110) :

"For you, ungrateful boy, I keep my treasures all, and no one shall enjoy them but yourself; my mentula is growing: while it used to measure seven inches, now it measures ten."

Elegy IV, to Marcus (p. 113) :

"You could not, Marcus, find a better, a more convenient, place, in which to meet me; not a spy is here nor witness, neither man nor woman can tell tales. Let's do it under the willows in this verdant meadow; the drooping boughs will hide us with their foliage. The rivulet will lull us to sleep with its pleasant murmur, and the bird that warbles mid the boughs. Hither come, and glide into my lap, thou that art torment at once and remedy of my desires!"

Elegy XIV (p. 128) :

"One day Etruscus brought to me a youth, so fair as is seldom seen at Jupiter's board: "I give him up to you", he said, "lay hold of "him, that he may cling to you both day and "night. May the gods grant you love him "well; he will be wise if you but pedicate "him.""

And I: "I like this liberty conceded to my "passion; I shall always be obliged to you. Be "sure this child, good as he is, will be better "still in future; he will suck my wisdom in "through many places."

Joyful he goes, joyful I seize hold of my prey; delay, however short, seems long to me. Oh, father proved in virtue! the one blameless man, the one sage in this great town! The master lays hands upon the lad's posteriors, the lad grasps the master's member. Think you, ye unlearned, he will learn in this fashion? Oh, lucky boy, to have me for a teacher! oh lucky fate, that gave you such a father!"

Elegy XV (p. 131):

"If the member is dead, the voluptuous wish is still alive; if the old man can no longer pedicate, he still wants to."

Elegy XX (p. 139):

"My member is so little, this part of me so dwindled, I almost think I never had one, or that it has disappeared; my finger cannot feel, my eye cannot see it,—fate has been but niggardly to me. I could be your attendant, Cybelé, without operation, I need no shard of glass, I am a castrated priest already. And still—it is a shame, but must be confessed; there is no worser lad than I in all the world. As soon as ever I could, I served the filthy Venus, for the hand of Pederasts had drawn me to it; a thousand members and big ones, churned in my inside, and day and night my anus was in quest. If only my passive action could have profited my member, when erect it would have touched my head, when limp my feet; but nothing did it good, it never grew. And what I did, perhaps only made it worse. Every boy likes to see his member grow, get big enough to amply fill his hand."

But enough of pedication; irrumation is our next business.

CHAPTER III

OF IRRUMATION (57)

TO put the member in erection into another's mouth is called to *irrumate,* a word, which in its proper sense means to give the breast; in fact, according to *Nonius,* p. 579 (Gottfried's edition), the Ancients called the bosom *ruma.* The verge, introduced into the mouth, wants to be tickled either by the lips or the tongue, and sucked; the party who does this service to the penis is a fellator or sucker, for with the Ancients *fellare* meant to suck, also according to *Nonius,* p. 547. The equivalent to *fellare* in Greek is————,

The Lesbians are believed to be the inven-

---

(57) You see we follow the same general order as in the *Priapeia,* VII.

"*I* warn you, boy, I mean to pedicate you; with you, my girl, I will copulate. The *third* penalty is kept for the bearded ruffian."

tors of this particular nastiness. The Scholiast, in verse 1337 of the *Wasps* of Aristophanes, cites Theopompus as vouching for the fact.

This is the reason why the Greeks apply the expression "Lesbianize" or "Lesbize" to those who imitated the Lesbian usages, either as *irrumants,* or as *fellators.* Suidas: "Lesbianize—to defile the mouth; the Lesbians are in fact believed to give themselves to these shameful acts." The same author says under the word, *"Siphnianize,—*to *Lesbianize,* that is to use the mouth abominably (58)" Aristophanes has employed the word in the sense of *sucking (Wasps,* 1337).

"Look, how cleverly I kept you away, when you wanted to Lesbianize the guests."

And again in the *Frogs* 1343:

"Has this Muse never used the Lesbian mode? (59)"

---

(58) Eustathius, p. 741, is very ambiguous: "Lesbianize,—to commit a shameful action."

(59) I do not quite know whether the following passage from the *Thesmophoriaeusae* (915-917) refers to this or no:

"Now, unhappy girl, you long for pleasure after the Ionian mode. Besides I think you are a Labda, as is the way of the Lesbians."

But Hesychius has employed it for *irrumate*: "Lesbianize, to defile a man's mouth".

Lesbianize and Phoenicianize are generally used conjointly, as though this practice had been equally common among the Phoenicians. Lucian says in his *Apophras* (ch. 26):

"In the name of the Gods tell me what you are thinking of, when it is bruited about publicly that you Lesbianize and Phoenicianize?"

What the difference between the two may be is not known. At any rate Timarchus, who is so bitterly attacked by Lucian, was a *fellator,* as may be readily gathered from the following. Timarchus, having arrived at Cyzicus to be present at a wedding feast, was turned out of doors (*ibid.,* ch. 26), the mistress of the house upbraiding him in these words

---

A fellatrix seems to have borne the name of landa, by reason of the first letter of the word Lesbianize: but the passage stands quite isolated, for in that of Varro, preserved by Nonius, and referring to the annotation of Scaliger on the Priapeia LXXVIII, where we find:

"Depsistis, decite. Labdae."

The reading is doubtful, and the sense note clear. The verse of Ausonius, Epigr. 128:

"When he puts his tongue in, then he is a Labda," has nothing to do with this question, as we shall show later on.

for the impurity of his mouth: "I would not have in my house a man who must have a man himself!" The passage preceding the above is still plainer and more to the point: What does the man reproach Timarchus with, who has surprised him kneeling before a young lad (*ibid.,* chap. 21), and who says farther on, "that he had seen him at work", if this does not apply to a *fellator*? Besides, what is the meaning of that sore throat contracted by him in Egypt (*ibid.,* ch. 27), where according to rumour, he had been nearly suffocated by a sailor, who fell upon him and stopped his mouth? Whence that nickname of the Cyclops (*ibid.,* ch. 28), which was given to him, because one day, when he was lying drunk on the ground, a young man, "with an upstanding stake exceeding well sharpened", threw himself upon him, to force it into his mouth, as Ulysses did with the eye of the Cyclops, "A new Cyclops, with the mouth open at full stretch, you let him burst your cheeks". It is useless to add to this the passages with respect to those who repel his kisses (ch. 23), or as to the use to which he puts his tongue (ch. 25), for it is doubtful whether they are addressed

to a *fellator* or a *cunnilingue* (a licker of the
vulva). That Timarchus was no stranger to
irrumation, seems implied (ch. 17) by the
apostrophe, "Are you not all that?" the more
so as previously Lucian's saying: "If any one
sees a cinede do or suffer the shameful act..."
makes it apparent that the active part was also
one of the vices of Timarchus. Lucian could
therefore justly say of this Timarchus, that he
Lesbianized and Phoenicianized, if he wanted
to imply by one of these words, "sucking", and
by the other, "irrumating." But it is uncertain
which of these words means "to suck", and
which "to irrumate". But what does this matter? There is no doubt that Lucian intended
to make this distinction. Phoenicianize might
even be applied to a *cunnilingue* (60), an expression which we shall dilate upon presently.
Needless therefore in this place to give ex-

---

(60) I do not know whether the nickname of Rododaphné (rose-laurel), given to Timarchus in Syria (ibid,
ch. 27), does not mean *cunnilingue,* as by rose is understood the female parts, while the laurel leafs means the
licking tongue. This surname had no doubt for Lucian
an obscene sense which he would not disclose: "In Syria
they call you Rododaphné, why? I should blush to say
it."

amples of women who allowed their vulvas to be licked.

Very remarkable is a passage of Galen in book X, *De vi simplicium,* in which he makes a distinction between Lesbianize and Phoenicianize, demonstrating that the one is more shameful than the other:

"It is worse for an honest . ıan to be spoken of as an eater of excrements than as being a defiler or a cinede; and amongst the defilers we execrate such as Phoenicianize more than those who Lesbianize. The latter I consider to be doing what is as bad as the habit of drinking menstrual discharge (61)."

Galen means by this that the man who uses human excrements as medicine is considered worse than a fellator or a cinede; that amongst the fellators the Phoenicianists are more

---

(61) Here is the preceding sentence, which will better elucidate Galen's meaning: To drink sweat, urine or menses is an abominable and detestable practice; human excrements still more so, in spite of what Xenocrates has written about their beneficial action when applied in lieu of ointment about the mouth or throat, or when swallowed. He has also spoken of the absorption through the mouth of ear-wax. I myself could not make up my mind to eat of them, though it were to cure my sickness right off. Of all abominable things the most abominable, I think, are human excrements.

abominable than the Lesbianists. There can
therefore be no doubt that he designates the
action of the *fellators* by the word Phoenician-
izing, and by Lesbianizing that of the *irrumants*. In fact, as he judges those the worst
who come nearest to the eaters of excrements,
he could not detest less those who defile their
mouths by fellation than those who defile the
mouths of other people by irrumation; similarly he could not help holding in abhorrence
the *cunnilingues* and the drinkers of menses,
of whom more later on.

But the Lesbians found imitators. The inhabitants of Nola were in bad repute amongst
the Ancients in that respect; in Ausonius,
Epigr. LXXI, Crispa, a fellatrix, is said to
practice the business "with which an unprecedented effeminacy inspired the people of
Nola". However, here is this spirited epigram in its entirety:

"Over and above the intimate joys of legitimate love, hateful lust has found out other
foul modes of pleasure, of the sort the loneli-
ness of Lesbos taught Hercules' heir, of the
sort smooth tongued Afranius in his actor's
gown displayed upon the stage, of the sort an

unprecedented effeminacy inspired the men of Nola with. Crispa, with but one body, yet practises them all: masturbates, fellates, works by either orifice,—dreading to die in vain before she has tried every mode."

To explain,—of course Crispa did not neglect to have herself entered in the usual way; these are "the intimate joys of legitimate love" Then she allowed herself to be pedicated; this is the vice of Philoctetes, the inheritor of the arrows of Hercules, as also Afranius, of whom Quintilian says: "He excelled in the Roman comedy; a pity that he polluted his plays with infamous masculine amours! He thus bore witness against his own morals" (*Inst. Orat.,* X, I). Further Crispa did not fail to allow herself to be *irrumated,* this is, "the vice their unprecedented effeminacy instilled into the men of Nola". Lastly the whole is recapitulated quite plainly in the last line but one; to masturbate is the genus, while to fellate, and to work by one and the orther orifices are so many species, three altogether.

There are authors who think that the celebrated riddle of Coelius in Quintilian: *Clytaemnestram quadrantariam, in triclinio coam,*

in cubiculo nolam (*Instit. Orat.*, VIII, 6 p,
747), refers to a woman of the name of Nola,
she being a *fellatrix* after the fashion of the
Nolans. But I prefer the interpretation of Al-
ciatus; he believes that the woman in question
was Clodia, the notorious sister of Clodius,
and wife of Metellus, called *Coa,* because she
liked coitus on the open triclinium, and *Nola*
because she refused the same in bed. Spald-
ing evinces surprise at the want of exactitude,
which the word *quadrantaria* would have in
that case. To me that appears like looking for
knots in a rush. Why should we not suppose
Clodia, disgusted, like Messalina, by the facil-
ity of her adulteries, to have been drawn into
extraordinary excesses (62) to such a point
that she would no longer have commerce with
men in the dark, but only in the glare of lighted torches, as Martial confesses in speaking of
himself (XI, 104):

"You love the game in the dark, I like it by
lamp-light; my delight is to make my entry
with light to see by,"—and in the presence of
living witness, that she might be seen, if not

---

(62) Tacitus, *Annals,* XI, 26.

actually on her back, at any rate going away for it or just coming back afterwards. Do you think that indecency could not possibly go so far? What did Augustus do, whom Marc Anthony, according to Suetonius, "reproached for having at a festival taken the wife of a Consular from the triclinium to a bedroom, in the presence of her husband, and afterwards conducted her back to the table with her face all on fire and her hair in disorder?" (*Augustus,* ch. 69). And Caligula, according to the same Suetonius, "when a guest at a wedding-feast said to Piso, who was sitting close by him: "Do not push up so close to my wife!" and immediately after made her rise from the table and took her away with him" (*Calig.,* ch. 25). The same author, (*Calig.,* ch. 36), speaking of the most illustrious Roman ladies, tells us that Caligula "invited them to dinner with their husbands, passing them in review before him, he examined them with the minute attention of a slave dealer, lifting their heads up if any of them bowed them down with shame. As often as he felt inclined, he left the triclinium and took the chosen fair one aside with him; then after returning to the room with the traces of his doing still upon him, he would praise or criticize these ladies openly, speaking of the beauties or blemishes of their bodies, and even how often he had repeated the enjoyment." Horace again speaks of an adulterous woman (*Odes,* III, vi, 25-32) :

"Soon she looks out for fresher adulterous pleasures, while the husband is drunk; and does not care to whom she grants the furtive forbidden pleasures, which with the torches extinguished, she is ready to give and take. Nay! she does not care for her very husband's presence, and with his knowledge she rises to meet whosoever may call, say a merchant, say the commander of a Spanish ship in harbour, who buys her favours by tariff!"

Again look at the feast of the Pope, Alexander VI, whom we have already mentioned for your profit and amusement in our *Hermaphroditus* (63).

_____

(63) We will here reproduce the curious passage of Jean Burchard, to whom we owe this story. It is taken from his *Diarium,* edited by Leibnitz, in 1696, p. 77:

"On the last Sunday in October the Duke of Valentinois had invited to supper in his chamber" (the chamber of Alexander VI), "in the Apostolical palace, fifty beautiful prostitutes, called courtezans, who, after supper

Is this evidence enough to satisfy you as to these *Coae* of the triclinium? Well! it was after this fashion Clodia preferred to be had. Alone with a solitary lover in bed and no one by, she refused (*nolebat*) ; in public on the triclinium, she was willing enough for coition (*volebat coire*). Hence the jest; she was *Coa* and *Nola*. Coelius might have put it still more plainly; on the triclinium she was *Vola,* in bed *Nola*.

It was not the inhabitants of Nola only who were addicted to the Lesbian vice, the Oscans (64) generally were considered to be very

---

danced with the valets and other persons present, first in their clothes, and then naked. After this the table, chandeliers were placed on the floor here and there, with lighted candles, and chestnuts were thrown about, which the courtezans collected moving on their hands and knees quite naked among the chandeliers, the Pope, the Duke and his sister Lucrezia being present and looking on. Finally presents were brought in: silk mantles, pairs of shoes, head-dresses, and other objects, to be given to those who had copulated with the greatest number of these courtesans: they were publicly enjoyed in the room there, the lookers-on acting as umpires, and awarding the prizes to the victors."

(64) Nola was a city in the territory of the Campanians. It is for this reason that the *Campanian malady,* mentioned by Horace (Sat. I., V., 62), has been connected with debauchery, but without sufficient reason.

much given that way, so much so that certain authors trace to them (the Osci), in earlier times called the Opsci or Opici, the etymology of the word "Obscene", Festus, p. 553:

"In almost all the old treatises the word is written *Opicum* instead of *Oscum;* it is from the name of this people that shameless and impudent expressions are called obscene, because indulgence in filthy debauchery was very common among the Oscans."

The Ancients employed many forms of circumlocution to convey the meaning of their filthy practices. For instance, instead of *irrumate,* they said: to offend the mouth (65), corrupt the mouth (66), to attack the head (67), to defy to the face (68), insult the head, not to spare the head (69), to split open the mouth

---

(65) Varro, is his *Marcipor,* according to Nonius: "He introduced afterwards into his gullet the virile verge: he offends the mouth of Volumnus."

(66) Martial III, 75:

"You make it your work to corrupt pure lips for gold."

And Again II, 28:

"Not even Vetustilla's warm mouth give you more pleasure."

(67) "How accustomed he was to assault the heads of

(70), gain the heights (71), mount to loftier

the most illustrious women, is plainly evidenced by the adventure of Mallonia, who, debauched by him, refused to submit to him again. He caused her to be accused by his informers, and kept asking her during her trial, whether she had anything to reproach herself with. Without waiting for the verdict, she ran home and transfixed herself with a poniard, upbraiding loudly the foul, hairy dotard for having wanted to abuse her mouth (Suetonius, *Tiberius,* ch. 45).

(68) He was so glad to have won Transalpine Gaul that he could not help announcing some days after in the Senate, that he had reached the fulfillment of his wishes, in spite of the hatred and malice of his enemies, and that he defied them to their face. Somebody having said to him offensively that this could not so easily be done with a woman, he replied jokingly, that Semiramis had gained a kingdom, and the Amazons had occupied a great part of Asia (Suetonius, *Caesar,* ch. 22). Caesar employed the expression: "defying to the face" in the honest sense, while his adversary invested it with an obscene signification, in allusion to his infamous acts in Bithynia.

(69) I speak of those whose abominable lasciviousness and execrable lust do not even spare the head. (Lactantius, *Instit. Div.* VI., 23.) Similarly **Juvenal VI., v.** 299, 300:

"For what cares the drunken Venus? She knows not the difference between groin and head."

(70) Martial II, 72:

"They say Posthumus, that they did to you last night, at supper, what I would not have let them do;—who could approve such doings? They split your mouth!..."

regions (72), compress the tongue (73), to in-

Then playing upon the words rumour and irrumate he adds:

"....As the author of this crime, the town's rumour designates Caecilius."

And again III, 73, ibid.:

"Rumour denies you are a Cinede".

III, 80:

"Rumour says, you have an evil tongue."

And III, 87:

"Rumour says, Chioné, that your vulva is intact, that nothing could be purer than it. Yet you bathe without covering the thing that should be covered; if you have any shame, then put your drawers upon your face."

Percidere employed alone means to pedicate. Martial IV, 48; VII, 61; IX, 48; XI, 29; XII, 35; and Priapeia, XII, XIV. Some copies have *praecidere* for *percidere,* but this seems to be an untenable reading.

(71) Martial, XI, 47:

"Why do you plague in vain unhappy vulvas and posteriors; gain but the heights, for there any old member revives."

Priapeia LXXV:

"Through the middle of boys and girls travels the member; when it meets bearded chins then it aspires to the heights."

(72) Priapeia XXVII:

"A footlong amulet will pedicate you; if that will not cure you, I go higher."

(73) Plautus, in the *Amphytrion,* I sc. 1, 192:

dulge in abominable intercourse (74), and instead of receiving the member into the mouth they said: to lend the mouth in kind complaisance (75), work with the mouth (76), lick

---

"I shall compress to-day the wicked tongue."

The Latins employed the verb "compress" for *irrumate,* as if it were a form of fornication; and similarly "split open", as if it were a form of pedication.

(74) Plutarch: "It is reported that in the night before the passing of the Rubicon, Caesar had a frightful dream; he dreamt that he was indulging in abominable intercourse with his mother." (*Lives, Julius Cæsar,* XXXII.) Hesychius' interpretation refers to this:— to perform abominable acts."

(75) Suetonius: "A picture of Parrhasius, representing Atalanta in the act of complacently lending her mouth to Meleager was bequeathed to him with the alternative that he might have a million sesterces instead, if the subject offended him. He not only preferred the picture, but had it solemnly hung in his bedroom. (*Tiberius,* ch. 44.)

(76) Horace, *Epode* VIII, 17-20:

"The member of the uneducated is it less rigid? does it not long, like those of lettered men? To make it stand superbly from the groin, you need but to work it with your mouth."

men's middle parts (77), lick simply (78), or

---

(77) Martial II, 62:
"A doubtful down did scarcely deck your cheek, when your tongue already licked men's middle parts." The same III, 81:
"Baeticus, you, a Gaul, what have you to do with the female pit? that tongue of yours should lick men's middles."
Ausonius, *Epigr.* CXX:
"When Castor longed in vain to lick men's middles, but could take no one home with him, he found means not to lose all pleasure of the sort, fellator as he was; he started to lick his own wife's organs." In other words from being a *fellator* Castor became a *cunnilingue*.
(78) Martial III, 88:
"They are twin brothers, but they suck different teats: tell me are they more unlike or like?"
The one was a *fellator,* the other a *cunnilingue*.
"Again, VII, 54:
"You shall suck not mine, which is honest and small, but a member escaped from the fire of Solyma's city and condemned to tribute."
I do not know whence Scioppius (*Priap.* X), has it, that Martial was well furnished; the latter avows in that passage, that his mentula was quite small. To affront Chrestus, he orders him to lick, not his, but the mentula of a Jewish slave. He has mentioned this Jewish slave already in Epig. 34 of the same book:
"My slave carries a heavy Jewish parcel without skin to cover it." That means his member is circumcised, the gland being uncovered, without prepuce, in one word, "reculitus." So, I think, is to be understood the *recutitorum inguine virorum* of Martial (VII, 29): he means, "the virile parts of circumcised men," the skin of whose glands is drawn back. *Recutitus* stands for *re-*

lastly to be silent (79). Just as Persius has

cinctus, regelatus, reseratus. Many other words, e.g.
revincire, similarly admit of two meaning, and thus, no
doubt should arise about Martial's expression: *recutita
colla mulae* (IX, 58), which refers to the mules having a
new skin covering their necks. I differ from those who
think that those were called *recutiti* whose prepuce began to grow again; a *recutitus* was to the Romans an
object of contempt. Petronius: "He has two faults, else
he would be like any other man *recutitus est et sertit.* He
is circumcised and snores" (*Satyr.,* ch. 28). It is impossible to suppose the *glans* could have been thought more
disgusting covered by a new prepuce than with none at
all.

(79) A man that is being irrumated cannot speak, his
mouth being obstructed by the mentula, thus: he is silent. Martial (III, 96) says to Gargilius, a *cunnilingue,*
menacing him with the third punishment, if he should
catch him in the fact:
"If I should catch thee at it, Gargilius, I'll make thee
silent."
Married men were in the habit of pedicating beardless
adults, and of irrumating the bearded ones. For which
reason Martial warns Gallus (II, 47) to shun the seduc-
tions of a famous rakish lady, as he was running the
risk, if taken by the husband in flagrante delicto, of
being irrumated by him:
"Your buttocks you rely on? But the husband is no
pederast; he likes but two ways, either mouth or vulva."
And for the same reason he consents to *marry* Thelesina (II, 49):
"No Thelesina for me as my wife! Why?—She is a
prostitute. Nay! but she pays young lads. Then I consent."
Then there is a complaint for having been deceived
with respect to the lover of Polla, his mistress (X, 40):

employed the word *cevere,* to wriggle in the
sense of flattering, so Catullus uses *irrumate*
as meaning to treat ignominiously (80).

"Constantly was I told that my Polla was on intimate
terms with an unknown cinede. Well, I surprise them,
Lupus; no cinede was he."

Instead of a lad, whom he would have pedicated, he
finds a cool, experienced gallant, not at all likely to expi-
ate his crime by means of his buttocks. Martial might,
however, have punished him more cruelly by forcing into
his fundament, either a mullet (Juvenal X, 317):

"There are adulterers whom the mullet pierces"; or a
radish. "In Armenia, taken in the act of adultery, he ran
away plugged with a radish in his posteriors." (Lucian,
De Morte Peregrini,—Works, vol. VII, p. 425.) Catullus XV, 18, 19:

"Drawing your feet asunder, your postern wide open,
they will insert into you radish and. mullet."

Martial also has used the expression of *being silent,* in
the above stated sense but, somewhat more obscurely, IX,
5:

"If in two apertures you can work, Galla, and can do
more than double work in both, why, Aeschylus, does she
get tenfold pay? She fellates, but that is not a matter of
such price surely. Nay! it is because she must be silent!"

It is not her infamy that Galla sells so dear; it is the
inconvenience of having to be silent during the process,
which, for a prattler, "is a very serious matter," as Martial says, IV, 81. Book XII, *Epigr.* 35, quoted later on,
also refers to this.

(80) It is the same with the word *stuprum.* Festus:
The ancients employed the word stuprum for turpitude,
as appears in the Song of Neleus.

"Foede stupreque castigor cotidie."

It is thus he complains of having been irrumated by Memmius XXVIII., 9, 10:

"Oh, Memmius, well and long and leisure-
ly, laid on my back all the length of that beam,
you irrumated me."

He had, in fact, experienced in Bithynia the
meanness and avarice of this Praetor, Memmius, who had not cared a rap for his com-
rades' honour, and who is alluded to in Epigr.
X., 12, "Praetor and irrumator". In Epigr.
XXXVII., he threatens his boon companions
in debauchery, with whom his mistress has
taken refuge:

".... Do you think I dare not irrumate
alone, as I stand here, two hundred pothouse-
heroes?" And he adds that he would write on
the front of the tavern the infamy of these
blackguards:

".... Your names I shall chalk up all over
the tavern's front."

Other passages of Catullus, XXI., 12, and
LXXIV., 5, are also quoted to prove the various employment of the word *irrumate;* but

---

(I am foully and disgracefully beaten every day.)
Naevius: "They would rather die than return to their
co-citizens *cum stupro*".

they do not seem to me to bear upon the question.

The epithet *shameless* was especially given to the man who allowed himself to be pedicated or irrumated. *Priapeia* LIX.:

"If you come to steal, you will return *shameless.*"

Cicero, *DeOratore,* II., 257:

"If you are *shameless* before and behind..."
Horace, *Epistle,* I., xvi., 36:

"If he calls me a thief, he denies that I am chaste."

Lampridius, *Commodus,* ch. 10:

"Already as a child he was a glutton and *shameless,* which is explained by what he says in chap. 5: "He gave himself up to the infamous abuses of young men and to their assaults", and chap. i: "From his tenderest age he was depraved, mischievous, cruel, a libertine; he allowed his mouth to be soiled and defiled."

On the other hand, a woman who had never submitted to a man, was called *chaste* (*Priapeia* XXXI.):

"You are allowed to be as chaste as Vesta;"
The same epithet was given to a wife that was

faithful to her husband such a one as is praised by Martial in *Epigr.* X., 63.

"My couch is lighted by the rarest glory,—one member, one mentula alone has known my chastity."

To the preceding examples of *fellators* and *fellatrices* we will now add, from Aloysia Sigaea's book, that of Crisogono, who cleverly persuades Sempronia to lend him her mouth:

"The day before yesterday (it is Ottavia speaking), Crisogono came to see my mother in the afternoon. All was quiet and silent. He had scarcely begun to wanton a little with her, when he became very importunate. "Yesterday morning", he said, "I learned a new kind of pleasure. One of our grand personages, who had certainly tasted it, says that there is nothing so disgusting and repulsive as those parts of his wife which stamp her as a woman,—and he has a very pretty wife, mind! In that sink every thing is foul, while in this (kissing my mother on the mouth), dwells the true Venus. He therefore abominates that illfavoured cavern, and adores that pure mouth, that charming head. He looks to nothing else, his member rises for nothing else. His wife is as spirit-

ed as she is beautiful, and even more obliging.
She knows no other pleasure than her husband's; what he thinks right she thinks proper,
and abets all the caprices of her husband; so
she lends him the service of her mouth. What
would you do, Sempronia, if I asked you? If
you were to refuse I should say that you have
forgotten all your promises and your pledged
faith. You know that Socrates said, the beautiful body of a pretty woman is nothing but a
living treasure chamber of voluptuousness, the
storehouse whereto men resort to find their
pleasures, whereto they direct the burning
floods of their lubricity. "What matter whether you fulfil your duty through that pure canal
(kissing her mouth), or through that other
(touching below), which is infect?" He per-
suaded her to what she was willing to do without persuasion. "Oh!" she said, smiling,
"what an air you want me to play, and upon
what a flute, in our concert!" taking in her
hand his member, which began to rise. She
seized the point of his dart between her lips
and turning her tongue around it, caused novel
transports of delight to the member that slid
into its new receptacle. But feeling that the

fountains of the brine of Venus were on the point of bursting forth, she recoiled with horror. "You would not degrade me so far", said my mother, "as to make me drink a man in a liquid form?" She had scarcely spoken, when an abundant shower fell upon her robe. He showed some anger, "How could you be so foolish," he cried, "as to spoil such good work!" She replied: "Forgive me, the next time you will find me more obelient." She kept her word, and actually drank men in a liquid state,—a spicy thing, for indeed the seed is spicy with salt!" (Dial. VII.)

Mancia also proved complaisent in that way to Marino; Eleanor tells it in Aloysia Sigaea:

"My cousin, Mancia, has married a Neapolitan of the name of Marino. Marino is burning all over with debauchery. The libertine looks for the woman in Mancia even above the breasts; he wants her mouth, as though the vulva of the young wife had taken refuge there, or as if the mouth had made a bargain with the vulva to participate in the games of Venus. I blamed her for allowing so unnatural an act. "What would you have?"she said. Marino's instrument occupies my mouth, so I cannot complain. We please our husbands only by reason of being women. Never mind where she is taken, if a woman only proves that she is a woman, she will please." (Dial. VII.)

So too Alfonso tries to engage Eleanor herself in the same fashion:

"Look you! Ottavia", added Eleanor, how passionately loving Alfonso is. Some days ago, after having several times plied his javelin in the legitimate way, he presented it to my mouth. "Your catapult, my Alfonso", said I, "is not made for breaching this door; you are mad, and you want to make me the same." "No! I would fain have you mad, not myself; for that you love me, I owe to your madness, not to any merits of my own. If I get delirious, I may forget the respect which I owe you, and I would rather die than cease to live for you alone." These words softened my heart, and decided me to assist him in that game. I seized his inflamed dart with a good heart between my lips. But that was all, his member returned voluntarily to the place it had left, and finished its exploits, which it had impudently begun

above, properly in the region of the middle."
(Dial. VII.)

Gonzalvo of Cordova was another amateur
of this mode. Aloysia Sigaea:

"Gonzalvo of Cordova, a celebrated general, is said to have taken very much to this
kind of voluptuousness in his old age." (Dial.
VII.)

The prurient ingenuity of Tiberius invented a new species of *fellation*.

"His turpitude went still farther, to such infamous excesses, that it is as difficult to relate
them as to listen to them; they are scarcely
credible. He caused little children, of the ten-
drest age to be taught to play between his legs,
while he was swimming in his bath, calling
them his little fishes, to touch him lightly with
tongue and teeth, and like babies of some little
strength and growth, though not yet weaned,
to suck his privates as they would their mother's breast. His age and his inclination predis-
posed him for this sort of pleasure before all
others." (Suetonius, *Tiberius,* ch. 44).

A representation of this ingenious libertine
while tickled by what he called his little fish-

es, is to be seen on plate XVIII. of the *Monuments de la vie privée des douze Césars.*

Men advanced in age, whose member will no longer obey their will, are more inclined to irrumate than others. To this circumstance the passage in Martial, IV., 50, refers:

"No man is too old to irrumate."

XI., 47:

"Gain the heights; there your old member will revive."

And III., 75:

"Your mentula, Lupercus, has long ceased to stiffen; nevertheless, in your folly you strive to make it rise. You are fain now to corrupt pure lips for gold; but even so your Venus is stimulated in vain."

For this reason irrumators are less feared by married men. Thus Martial dealt more lightly with Lupus, whom he had surprised while irrumating his Polla, in the passage (X., 40) quoted previously. The husband of Glycera, if so be that she had one, also need not have feared that Lupercus would do duty for him, Martial, XI., 41:

"Lupercus loves the beautiful Glycera; he is her lord and master, and he alone. He was complaining bitterly he had not loved her for a month; Aelianus asked the reason,—he replied Glycera had the toothache."

Lepidinius, in the *Hermaphroditus* (I., 13), is of opinion, that anyone who has once irrumated can never get rid or renounce the habit. I must leave it to experts to decide upon this. So also thinks Aloysia Sigaea: "Such as have once tasted it, are mad after this pleasure." (Dial. VII.)

No wonder that after fellation, the mouth has to be washed out with water. Martial alludes to this, II., 50;

"You lend your mouth, and then drink water, Lesbia; quite right, — where your work is, there you take water."

Priapeia, XXX., says:

"Walk in the vineyards, and if you steal any of the grapes, you shall have water, stranger, to take in another way."

Priapus means: "You came to get water to drink; but if you pluck any grapes, I shall irrumate you, and then you will want water to rinse your mouth rather than to drink." Martial says as much to Chioné in *Epigram* III., 87, quoted before.

To ask for the loan of the mouth is to demand a thing much more shameful than the other two orifices. Martial, IX., 68:

"All the night long I possessed a lewd young girl; I never knew anyone more naughty. Tired of a thousand postures, I asked for the puerile service; before I had done asking, she turned at once in compliance. Laughing and blushing, I asked something worse than that,—the wanton consented instantly" (81).

---

(81) First the rogue lends her vulva, then her buttocks, and lastly her mouth. Some suppose the full-bosomed Spatalé of Martial (II, 52) was just as prodigal:

"Dasius was astute at counting the bathers; he asked full-bosomed Spatalé the fee of three women, and she paid."

But I believe they wrong the good Spatalé. Dasius, the bathing man, wanted only that Spatalé, whose charms were ample and buxom, she taking up as much room as three other women, should pay for three.

The Phyllis of Martial (XII, 65), showed herself liberal in every way:

"The beautiful Phyllis, who throughout the whole night had proved herself right liberal in every way...."

From this you will understand what Martial means by "refusing nothing" (XI, 50):

"I will not deny you anything, Phyllis; for you deny me nothing."

And similarly, IV. 12:

"You refuse no one, Thaïs. If you know no shame for this, blush at least that you refuse nothing, Thaïs!"

And again, XII, 72:

Those that found themselves thus situated took good care not to be surprised; Martial, XI., 46:

"When you have crossed the threshold of a chamber with name on signboard, whether it be boy or girl that smiled on you in welcome, doors and hangings and locks do not content you, and you want to be yet more certain you are not watched. Mystery is what you want; you look suspiciously on the smallest crack in the door and stop it; the same with the tiniest pinhole made by some inquisitive hand. Nobody can be more modest or circumspect in his doings, Cantharus, than the man who wants to pedicate or copulate."

"There is nothing, Lygdus, that you do not now deny me; there was a time when there was nothing you did deny!"

And he says (XII, 81) right out:

"Whoso refuses nothing, Atticilla, sucks."

It is in this sense that Mallonia refused to be entirely at the mercy of Tiberius; she had already admitted him to her vulva and anus, but when it came to the mouth the poor girl could not overcome her disgust. We have before quoted the passage of Suetonius. Of a woman who refuses nothing, Arnobius (II, 42) says: "That she is ready to undergo anything," and of a woman that is drunk, "so much so as not to able to refuse anything." Ovid says (*Art of Love,* III, v. 766):

"She is meet to undergo all kinds of assaults."

However, the old Romans did not blush to irrumate, as is evident by the use Catullus makes of that word, contemptuous though it be. What they *were* ashamed of was *fellation*. Indeed there is a certain bold audacity in playing the active part, but none in the passive one particularly when the mouth, the noblest organ of the body, has to perform such vile offices. Add to this that a fetid breath was acquired by this habit, which *fellators* took every means to hide, afraid of putting to flight fellow-guests at table and acquaintances who should greet them with a kiss in the street.

Fellators were so repugnant to the guests at table, that no cups (82) were offered to them,

---

(82) Martial, II, 15:
"You do not offer your cup to any man; it is discretion, Hermus, forbids, not pride."
And VI, 44:
"No one, Calliodorus may drink from your cup."
Seneca: When Caius Caesar accepted sums of money for the expense of the games from friends who brought them to him, he refused to take a large amount from Fabius Persicus. His friends not looking at the character of the sender, but at the value of the sum sent, reproached him for having refused. "What!" said he, "am I to accept the service of a man from whose cup I should decline to drink?" (*De Beneficiis,* II, 21.) Fabius Persicus was a *fellator* not a *cunnilingue;* this is apparent from the controversy in which Seneca engaged about

or when they had been offered, they were afterwards broken (83), and that it was only with the greatest unwillingness any one would kiss their mouth (84), when presented for salute. Thus it was preferable to be taken for a *cinede* to being taken for a *fellator* (85), like Phœbus in Martial, III., 73:

---

him, viz: what a prisoner should do whom a man promised to buy off, at the price of having his body prostituted, and his mouth sullied.

(83) Martial XII, 75:

"It is no little matter, Flaccus if you drink with them; and then have to break the cup they touched."

And Macedonius in the *Analecta* of Brunck, III, 116:

"There drank a woman with me yesterday, whose fame is anything but good;—go break the cups, my lads!"

(84) Martial XI, 96:

"Every time you happen to meet a *fellator's* kisses, I can fancy, O Flaccus, how you plunge your head in water."

And I, 95:

"You sung but badly, Agelé, when you were loved *per vulvam*. Now no one kisses you, and you sing well."

And I, 84:

"Your lap-dog, Manneia, licks your mouth and lips I am not a bit surprised; dogs like dirt."

Seneca: "And mark! he made that Fabius Persicus, whose kisses are shunned even by people who know no shame, a priest only the other day." (*De Beneficiis,* IV 30.)

(85) It appears from Martial's *Epigram* (XI, 99), that the kiss on the mouth was the regular thing with the

"You sleep with youths whose members are full size, and what rises with them, will not rise with you. Pray, Phœbus, tell me, what must I suspect? If I could think that you were but effeminate! But rumour says, you are not a *cinede*!"

The case of Callistratus, in XII., 35 of our author, is a similar one:

"You are very frank, Callistratus, with me, and you tell me that they often do it to you. You are not quite so simple, as you would appear; the man that tells such things does not tell of others worse (86)."

Romans; *fellators,* therefore, could not be surprised at their kisses being avoided. The poet of Bilbilis makes yet another mock at their expense (II, 42):

"Zoilus, why spoil the bath by bathing your bottom in it? If you would make it still dirtier, plunge your head in."

And VI, 81:

"You bathe, Charidemus, as though you had a grudge against mankind, entirely submerging in the bath your privates. I should not like you to wash your head that way, Charidemus; and now look! you are washing your head. I had rather it were your privates!"

(86) In the last verse there are two furtive stings; the first is about not telling (*tacet,* — is silent), an expression, which was used as denoting a *fellator;* the second is the word "tell," (*narrat*), the honourable use of the mouth being put for the dishonourable, as in Epistle III, 84:

For the same reason, as Charidemus will not be called a *patient,* and shows his legs and chest covered with hair. Martial tells him (VI., 56), to arrange himself in such a way as to appear a minion rather than a *fellator*:

"Because your legs are covered with bristles, your chest with hair, you think, Charidemus, to hand down your words to posterity; take my advice, and pluck the hair from all over your body, and get it certified you depilate your buttocks. Why so? you ask.—You know the world tells many tales; try to make them believe you are merely pedicated."

Fellation, as was but fair, received payment, and high payment. Martial (XI., 67) shows this:

"Informer you are and blackmailer, swindler and trickster, *fellator* and bully. The wonder is you have no money."

And again, III., 75:

"Your member, Lupercus, has long ceased to stiffen; nevertheless in your folly, you strive to make it rise. Of no avail is cole-wort or salacious onions, of no use to you the provo-

---

"What tells (*narrat*) your harlot.—No! I don't mean your girl, Tongilion! — What then? — Your tongue!"

cative savory. You are fain now to corrupt pure lips for gold; but even so your Venus is stimulated in vain. But,—a thing to be marvelled at and scarce believed,—what will not rise, Lupercus, does rise if you pay a heavy fee."

But when on the subject of fellation, we must not pass over in silence the raven, whom our standing authority (Martial, XIV., 74), calls a *fellator*:

"Saluting raven (87), why do they call thee *fellator?* Never a mentula entered your beak."

The fact is ignorant people believed the raven fulfilled the coitus with his beak:

Pliny says: "The vulgar herd believes that it operates the coitus and procreates with its beak. Aristole denied this, saying that ravens merely exchange kisses in the same way, familiar to everybody, that pigeons do." (*Natural History,* X., 12.)

---

(87) You will find in Macrobius (*Saturnalia,* II, 4), why he was called saluting. Augustus returned as victor from Actium; amongst those who came to congratulate him was a man holding a raven, which he had taught to cry: "I salute thee, Caesar Victor and Emperor!" Caesar, admiring this flattering bird, bought it for 20,000 secterces.

Erasmus denies in his *Adagia,* under the word *Lesbiari* (p. 409 of the Frankfort edition, 1670), that in his time the obscene practice of irrumation was still known:

"A**** (to lick), if I am not mistaken, is with the Greeks the same thing as *fellare* with the Latins. The word indeed remains; but the thing itself has been, I think, long done away with."

I fear this is not really the case. At any rate I am informed that this practice is not entirely opposed to the habits of libertines of the present day; those must decide whose opportunities take them to great cities. Plate XXI., in the *Monuments de la vie privée des douze Césars* represents a *fellator.* However the graceful picture in question really belongs more properly to the category of "spintrian poctures", of which more anon, than to the present chapter.

MANUAL

OF CLASSICAL EROTOLOGY

SECOND VOLUME

CHAPTER IV

OF MASTURBATION

T O excite the member by friction with the hand until the sperm comes spirting out of it is what the Ancients call masturbation, from *masturbare,* that is *manu stuprare,*—to pollute with the hand. This may be done by one's own hand, or by borrowing someone else's. If by one's own, it is generally the left hand that is employed, hence the expression, "left-hand whore" in Marital (IX., 42):

"You never, Ponticus, enter a woman, but use your left-hand whore, making your hand the mistress for your pleasure; think you this is nothing? Believe me, it's a crime, yes! a crime, and worse than you can imagine. Old Horatius copulated once at any rate to beget his three sons; Mars once to get chaste Ilia with twins. Neither of them could have done it, if by masturbation they had pro-

139

cured by the use of their own hand pleasures so shameful. Believe me, that nature's voice confirms it,—what escapes 'twixt your fingers, Ponticus, is a human being."

To the same subject also *Epig.*, XI., 74 refers:

"Oftentimes, Lygdé, you swear you will grant my prayer, even appointing the place, even appointing the hour. Longtime I lay consumed with longing, till often my left hand comes to help in your stead."

And this passage of the VIth. book of Ramusius, p. 62 of the Paris edition:

"What are you to do? Is your left hand safe and sound? Well use it, then you will not want a whore. Why pay for what your left hand gives you gratis?"

There were of course also people who used their right hand; the same Ramusius of Rimini, book IV., p. 61, tells us:

"I suffer, dear Donatus, from so frightful an erection, I am fearful for my member, if you do not help me. My right hand, being wounded, can do nothing; I have no money; Hylas is not here; no vulva opens for me— no chance of fornication, appease my desire, that I may live, and you can do it cheaply."

Pacificus Maximus, *Elegy* XII., p. 126,
Paris edition:

"What shall I do? I am so stiff—I'm
bursting, and I could easily fill three or four
large bottles. It is long since my member
has known a vulva, long since it has stirred
the entrails of a man. It is stiff day and
night, and will never relax,—night and day
it lifts its head. No youth, no girl will listen
to my prayer, no help—my right hand must
then do the service!"

We have seen just above, with what severity Martial reproached Ponticus, a masturbator, for losing between his fingers the
substance of a man. Nevertheless this fine
moralist did not hesitate to put his own
hand to similar use under the pressure of
erection, *Epigr.* 43, book II.:

"Another Ganymede, my hand assisted
me." and XI., 74:

"Often my left hand comes to my help in
your stead."

Nor was his severity given to whining
when he exhorted (XI., 59), the cinede
Telesphorus:

"Soon as ever you see I want it, and know that I am in erection, Telesphorus, then you demand a heavy price,—can I say nay (1)? If I will not swear to pay you, you will withdraw those posteriors of yours, which are so precious to me. If with his razor set to my throat my barber, whilst shaving me, demands my liberty and fortune, I promise all; 'tis not the barber asks, but a cut-throat, and fear compels me to say 'Yes.' But once I see the razor returned to its curved case and harmless, why! I will break every limb of the fellow. Not that I will harm you, but my left hand once washed, my member will say "Go hang! to your grasping avarice (2)."

---

(1) Martial had made use of the same interrogative phrase with the verb in the infinitive and *puta* put instead of *scilicet* also in Epigram III., 26. *Hoc me puta velle negare?* (Can I say nay to this?) Scholars have found occasion for a pile of annotations on the two passages: these need not detain us.

(2) Martial's meaning is: My left hand will console my suffering mentula; the business done, my hand covered with the ejaculation of the sperm, like the fleece on the pubis of Ravola in Juvenal (IX., 4),—if indeed it is the fleece of his pubis that is intended:

"Whilst Ravola with wet beard rubs the groin of Rhodopé" . . . the greedy cinede will be told to go to the

The same when his wife surprised him engaged with a youth (XI., 44),—a witty epigram quoted above, as also when he intended to marry Thelesina (II., 49) :

"Thelesina makes presents to young lads; all the better."

The same when he recommends somebody, I do not know who (XI., 23), to make use of the posteriors of Galesius only, as the part that would suit him;

"Youths are divided by nature; one part is reserved for girls, and the other for men— use your own portion."

Is what the pedicon loses in the anus of the cinede anything else but the substance of a man, which the masturbator wastes between his fingers?

As it is in the nature of the virile member to rise at the mere sight of a pretty woman's naked body, the amorous desire in that state

---

deuce, to slink off with drooping head, like the man in Horace (*Satires* II., 69), who finds:

"Nothing is left to him and his but to weep."

This moist hand reminds us of the adulterous woman in Juvenal (XI., 186), who:

"Show humid traces in the doubtful pleats of her tunic."

25
144 THE MANUAL

often craves imperiously for relief, for "man in erection is not overwise" (3). This is why, when the fair one's heavy coverlets have been thrown back:

"Meantime the adulterer she has sent for lurks in furtive concealment, and impatient of the delay, yet says never a word, but pulls his foreskin (4)."—Juvenal, VI., 236, 7. and why:

---

(3) Suidas under the word ******, after Aelius Dionysius apparently.

(4) It was not out of voluptuousness, but for decency's sake that Jews, who had renounced their nation, had their prepuce redressed over the gland, as they did not wish it to be seen that they had been circumcized, so they took means to get their bare gland recovered. "And they made for themselves new prepuces" (*Maccabees,* I., 1., 15), "Is there anyone that has been brought to believe, circumcized? Let him not recover his gland" (*Corinthians,* I., vii., 18). Celsus, *De Medicina,* VII., ch. 25: "If the gland is bare, and it is desired for convenience sake to recover it, this can be effected, but more easily with a child, than with a grown man, more easily with the man born so, than with the man who has been circumcized after the custom of certain people. After having explained the method of cure applicable to men, with whom it is a natural accident, Celsus continues: "With people that have been circumcized, the skin must be detached behind the crown of the gland. This operation is not very painful as the prepuce being loosened, you can draw it with the hand back to the pubis without any loss of blood.

"The Phrygian slaves would be masturbating behind the doors, each time his bride
mounted the Hectorean horse." — Martial,
XI., 105.

This is why during the dances of the young
Gaditanian girls, which were without doubt
very like the dances that are still so much
appreciated by the Spaniards (5), the limp

Then the loosened integument is drawn once more
over and beyond the gland. This done the verge is dipped
frequently into cold water, and then covered with a
plaster, which has a strong tendency to minimize inflammation. As soon as it is quite free from inflammation,
the verge is to be bandaged from the pubis to the annular
incision; the skin is then drawn over the gland, but kept
separate from it by a plaster. In this way the lower part
of the skin grows on again, while the upper part heals
without adhering." From this passage it would appear
that at the time of Celsus the method of laying bare the
gland which afterwards prevailed with the Jews was not
discovered yet, by which, according to Buxtorf (Diction-
naire Talmudique), after the prepuce has been cut away,
the circumcisor takes hold of the remaining skin between
the thin edges of his thumb nails, and draws it forcibly
back. If this practice had been customary it would have
been superfluous to separate the prepuce with the scalpel.
I conjecture from this, that the Jews were called *recutiti*
from having this skin of the gland drawn back, which, not
being done, the circumcision was not considered complete;
but Celsus makes me doubt this.

(5) Julius Caesar Scaliger, *Poetica,* book I., p. 64:
"One of these infamous dances was the * *** **

appendages of even grey-haired spectators begin to move visibly, as many authors tell us. Martial, VI., 71:

"Cunning in the wanton gestures that go with the Baetician castanets, skilled in dancing to the Gaditanian measures, she might well stiffen trembling Pelias, and excite Hecuba's husband to emulate vigorous Hector."

Juvenal, XI., 162-165:

"Perhaps you may wait while the Gaditanian dancer begins to feel the wanton stimulus of the loud strains of her accompanying band, and the girls, fired by the applause sink to the ground with quivering buttocks, —a sight to sting languid senses to love." (6)

---

meaning wriggling the haunches and thighs, the *crissare* of the Romans. In Spain this abominable practice is still performed in public.

(6) Do not miss, reader, the motive of this dance, with their buttocks wriggling the girls finally sunk to the ground, reclining on their backs, ready for the amorous contest. Different from this was the Lacedæmonian dance * ** * ** when the girls in their leaps touched their buttocks with their heels. Aristophanes in the *Lysistrata,* 82:

"Naked I dance, and beat my buttocks with my heels." Pollux, IV., ch. 24: "As to the * ** * **, this was a Laconian dance. There were prizes competed for, not only

But it is not only by the sight of a beautiful naked female the member is excited; who does not know that it is also roused merely by images called up by the imagination, particularly in the night. And the power of such fancies is such as to provoke a pleasurable ejaculation of sperm. Priapus himself has experienced this. *Priapeia* XLVIII:

"You see this organ after which I am called by my name Priapus, is wet; this moisture is not dew, nor yet hoar-frost. It is the outcome given of its own sweet will, on recalling memories of a complaisant maid."

It is said that Diogenes, the cynic, was a masturbator; once caught in the act of hand-

---

amongst the young men, but also amongst the young girls; the essence of these dances was to jump and touch the buttocks with the heels. The jumps were counted and credited to the dancers. They rose to a thousand in the ** *** * ! !"

Yet more difficult was that kind of dance which was called ****, in which the feet had to touch the shoulders. Pollux, *ibid.*: The **** were dances for women: they had to throw their feet higher than their shoulders."

This kind of dance is not unknown in more modern times. J. C. Scaliger, *Poetica,* book I., p. 651: "To this day the Spaniards touch the occiput and other parts of the body with their feet."

ling his mentula, he said: "I wish to heaven I could in the same way satisfy my stomach with friction when it barks for food." (7)

When the masturbation is done by the loan of another person's hand, it is possible that the pleasure is participated on the part of the agent.

It forms part of the business of a courtezan to be clever with her fingers; a languid member may by their use be invigorated. The inertness of the virile member may be caused by the inconveniences of age, and this either on the part of the woman, as in Martial, VI., 23:

"You require my penis, Lesbia, to be ever in erection for you; believe me a man's member is not like a finger. True, you strive to excite me with hands and tender words, but

---

(7) Diogenes Laertius, VI, 2, 46: "One day, whilst masturbating himself in the middle of the market he said: "I wish to heaven that I could prevent my stomach from being hungry by rubbing it." Plutarch, *De Stoicorum repugnantiis*, 1044, vol. II, of his works: "Chrysippus praised Diogenes for masturbating himself in public, and for saying to the bystanders: "Would to heaven by rubbing my stomach in the same fashion, I could satisfy my hunger."

your face is a stubborn fact and counteracts
all your efforts."

and again in the same author, XI., 30:

"When you set your old hand the task of
rousing my member, your thumb, my Phyllis,
will but strangle me."

or of the man, Martial, XI., 47:

"Only in dreams you get stiff (8), Maev-
ius, and your verge begins to make water
right onto your own feet; in vain your
wearied fingers ply your wrinkled member,
—rouse it as you may, it will not raise its
drooping head." (9)

Aristophanes in the *Wasps,* 735-38:

---

(8) Mark with what minuteness the Ancients scru-
tinized nature; with what ingenuity they gave expression
to all their sentiments! Who dares nowadays write such
a verse describing as a natural thing what might be but a
solecism of his mentula.

(9) Bassus, who was in the habit of taking his pleasures with young minions, longhaired and slim, set the
hands of his wife to work to excite his mentula, when he
came back to the conjugal couch fatigued and languid.
Martial, XII., 99:

"You tire yourself, oh Bassus, but with minions, paying
them from the dowry of your wife; thus when you return
to her side, that member bought at the price of many
million sesterces, lies languid. In vain her tender thumb
tries to excite it, vain are her tender words, it will not
stand."

"Yes, I will nurse him and get him all that is wanted for an old man: beef broth to lap, soft wool, and a rug to keep him warm, and a courtezan to rub his member and his loins . . ."

The same author, *ibid.,* v. 1334, 35:

". . . The cable is rotted away, yet is it still fond of being rubbed."

Nor is it unwelcome to men in the vigor of life, and who are fit to caress young girls, to have mistresses whose hands are not lazy in bed, and whose fingers know how to act in the dark regions where the arrow of love is hidden. Martial (XI., 105), complains about the unseemly gravity of his wife, which forbade her to render him that service:

"You will not help me on by movement or by word, nor yet with your fingers, as though you were preparing the incense and the wine for sacrifice (10)."

Penelopé, on the other hand, contented

---

(10) The women of Aristophanes (*Lysistrata,* v. 227) threatened their husbands with a similar rigidity of body:

"Though you may have your way, I shall be crabbed and never move."

Ulyses well that way, as Martial has it in the same epigram:

"Chaste though she was, when the king of Ithaca lay snoring, Penelopé liked to have her hand always on it."

Ovid's mistress did him the same service, but all in vain one miserable night, when a hostile divinity seemed to have smitten to death that most pitiful part of him, to use his own expression, and the girl, in order that the servants might not think that she had remained untouched, pretended to make her ablutions all the same (*Amores,* III., viii., 73, 74):

"My darling did not distain even to put her hand to it and gently try to rouse it."

This virtue of the fingers in procuring erection is alluded to by Juvenal (VI., 195, 96):

". . . How well a soft and libertine voice will erect your member; it is as good as fingers!"

The author of the *Priapeia* was also well aware of the fact; LXXX.:

"My member is not very long nor very

"My member is not very long nor very thick,—handle it, and you'll see it grow apace."

And so was Janus Dousa, quoted by Scioppius á propos of this same *Priapeia,* cleverly scenting out the man's character:

"Dousa, commenting upon Petronius, informs us that he knows *by home experience* how this object grows in thickness and length when shampooed by a woman."

You can estimate the importance of this function by the value set by the Ancients, as in our days by the Turks, upon shampooers, men and women, who are employed for manipulating the joints with artistic expertness, their fingers softly pressing and turning them, and their hands kept soft by the constant use of gloves, kneading tenderly all the limbs. Seneca, *Letter* LXVI.:

"Would I rather offer my limbs for shampooing to my superannuated minnons? or to some little woman, or some weakling man, more woman than man, to draw and crack my fingers? Should I not rather envy yonder Mucius, who put his hand in the fire with the same equanimity as though he tendered it to a shampooer."

Martial, III., 82:

"A woman shampoos your body all over with nimble skill; her trained hand manipulates *all* your members." (11)

John of Salisbury states in his *Policraticus,* book III, ch. 13, after some ancient author, perhaps Clearchus, as Lipsius thinks:

"When a rich libertine turns in his luxurious ways to effeminacy, a youth with frizzled hair takes before all the world his feet while he is lying on his couch, and shampoos them and his legs, not to go further, with his delicate hands. That youth is always wearing gloves, so as to preserve them white and soft for the benefit of rich people. Then, using his hands more licentiously, he runs them over all the body with impudent touchings and ticklings, raising the desires and stirring the amatory flames of his employer."

I may very well describe here, for I could not find a better place, a performance for which the friendly hand of a woman is in

(11) He had a hand of no less experience (Juvenal, VI., 422-23), that cunning shampooer who put his fingers to the lady's clitoris.

"And made his mistress's thigh resound beneath his hand high up."

request, but of a woman that is an expert, which will gently press your testicles and stroke your thighs; it is said that nothing can be pleasanter or more voluptuous. Aloysia Sigaea describes, with her inexhaustible ingenuity, such a scene, executed by Ottavia and Roberto, with the assistance of Manilia; the fullness, variety and richness of the description, placed in the mouth of Ottavia, are admirable:

"Manilia then conducted us to the trysting place; she undressed me, and placed me naked on the couch. Roberto jumped on to the couch. "Now," he said, "I shall enjoy the most supreme unalloyed bliss. Carried on your chariot, Olympia, I shall take my way through this dark thoroughfare (he was pinching my pubis the while), I shall take my way to glory." His hands were straying over my belly, my thighs, examining everything. His member was swelling. "Permit me, my Venus!" he said, giving me a kiss. "Willingly," I answered, "you shall have me in any way you like." Manilia interposed, "Why so much talk! Do not talk but act! I will assist both of you, and add new de-

lights to your voluptuous sensations. You
are in excellent trim, Roberto! Come, down
with you upon Ottavia's snowy bosom, and
have your fill!" Roberto precipitates himself upon me, and his engine strikes against
my belly. Manilia's soft hand intercepts the
erring tool. "Come," she says, "you vagrant,
enter the lovely prison, and do the task
set to you by your mistress." With her other
hand she pushes the young man's back, and
I take him in, entirely in. Manilia tells me
not to move. "Raise your left thigh, Ottavia," she says, "and stretch out the other one."
I obey. "You, Roberto, you now push gently
and quickly; As to you, Ottavia, kiss him
but without moving!" We do so. She added, "When you both feel the boiling foam
running over, you, Ottavia, give a sigh, and
you, Roberto, gently bite Ottavia's lips!"
He then begins to poke vigorously, but without haste or violence, in and out; I press him
on to me, kissing him but not moving. I
feel it coming. I sigh, "Now! now, Roberto!" cries Manilia, "help Ottavia! Work
away!" He shakes me and pounds me. Soon
I feel a slight bite on my neck. I heave a

sigh. "And now, Ottavia," cries Manilia, "you assist Roberto; move your buttocks briskly, raise up your loins, quick! quick! Well done, my child! "Laïs herself, I think, could not have shown more flexibility nor agility!" The sweet youth begins to ejaculate, and I feel my inside inundated by the fiery spring of love. I moved with body and soul. I never arrived more quickly at the acmé of voluptuousness. Manilia caressed with one hand my buttocks, and with the other hand Roberto's; at the same time she pressed with the points of her fingers the lips of my vulva and his testicles, which were close up. The youth swooned, and our nurse withdrew, and clapped her hands applauding!" (Dialogue VII.)

Plates IV. and XII., in the *Monuments de la vie privée des douze Césars,* show you Cleopatra titillating with a delicate hand the virile parts of Julius Cæsar and Mark Anthony, while in the *Monuments du culte secret des dames romaines;* plate XVI., represents Livia bestowing the same caresses on Augustus; plate V., a Bacchante doing it to a Faun; plate IV., a masturbator—expressly so called. In plate XLIV. of the *Monuments de la vie privée des douze Césars*, again, is a picture of a girl helping Tiberius with her benevolent hand in pedicating Otho.

Again it sometimes happened that lewd men found pleasure in handling the genital parts of other men. Martial knew nothing more infamous (XI., 23) :

"That your coarse lips should receive the delicate kisses of fair-skinned Galesus, that you should sleep with your naked Ganymede —is not this enough yet? It ought to be! Cease at any rate to touch the privates with provocative hand. With boys of tender age this does more harm than the member does. The fingers hasten virility and make them prematurely men. Hence the goaty smell, the quick-coming hairs, and the beard that make the mother wonder, while they no more love to bathe in the open light of day. Nature has divided boys; one part is reserved for girls, the other for men. Keep to the part which is yours."

Martial means to say that the member was given to boys for the purpose of using it with girls, while their buttocks were for the service of men, and that this pedicon should therefore make use of Galesus' buttocks rather than play with his mentula. Of similar import is also *Epigram* XI., 71, directed against Tucca, who wanted to sell young lads:

"Oh, for shame! there is the groin with the tunic all open, and a member appears fashioned and trained by your hand."

He says it is a crime to put up for sale those lads whom the infamous Tucca has trained for debauchery, and to let the buyers see their fully formed mentulas, accustomed to rise under the provocative hand of the master. Eumolpus subjects in the same way the verge of Encolpus to friction, Petronius, chap. 140:

"After these words" (Encolpus speaking) "I lifted up my tunic, and exhibited myself in full vigor to Eumolpus. He first recoiled as if horror-struck; but, like a man who expected worse, he got hold with his two hands of God's gift, viz.: the verge in erection."

I have still to treat, in order to complete my task, of other pleasures belonging to this category, meaning those which can be taken

in any interstice of the body. A few words
will suffice. Taking in the first place the
breasts, I have recourse to Aloysia Sigaea:

"By the twin conch-shells of Venus!" (Dialogue VII., Ottavia speaking.)   "I am
ashamed. I blush to think, that the valley
between my breasts has done duty as the
avenue of Venus. You know there is in
our house a gallery giving on the garden-
parterres, which are full of all sorts of flow-
ers. There Caviceo and I were promenad-
ing; he embraced me, kissed me, bit my lips.
. . . He put his left hand in my bosom. 'I
am after trying a naughty trick,' he said.
'Undress, my darling!' What was I to do?
I undressed. His eyes rested on my bare
bosom. 'I see,' he said, 'Venus sleeping between your breasts. May I waken her!'
While he was talking he had thrown me on
my back in the bed, and being in a noble
state of erection, slides his hot, burning member between my breasts. How could I escape his blind passion. I had no choice but
to bear it. His hands softly pressed my
breasts together, so as to narrow the space,
in which his mentula had to travel towards

a new experience. Why make a long story?
Stupefied as I was at this vain ridiculous
imitation of Love, he inundated me with a
burning libation: he had his will."

As to other interstices of the body, e. g. the
armpits, between the thighs, the calves, the
buttocks (mind, I do not say the anus, but
between the buttocks), be it enough to mention Heliogabalus; Lampridius, ch. 5:

"How put up with a Prince who sought
for pleasure in every cavity of the body,
when you would not suffer a brute beast to
do as much?"

Also Commodus, according to the same
Lampridius, ch. 5:

"He gave himself up to the infamous assaults of young men, polluting every part of
his body, even his mouth, and that with either
sex,"—i. e. he was both a *fellator* and a *cunnilingue.*

Is it necessary to speak here of the debauchery of those who assault the corpses of females, or statues? This is not real coitus,
there being no two parties to the act. Nevertheless, according to Herodotus (II., 89), in

Egypt a man was taken in the act of abusing the corpse of a woman just dead:

"It is said that a man was surprised in the act of working in the fresh corpse of a woman, and denounced by a fellow-workman."

In consequence of this a law was promulgated forbidding the corpses of noble and beautiful women to be given into the hands of the embalmer until three or four days after their decease. And who does not know the story of the Venus of Cnidos, the work of Praxiteles, as related by Pliny, *Historia Naturalis,* XXXVI., ch. 5:

"It is related how a certain youth fell in love with her, and having hidden himself one night in the temple, cohabited with the statue, leaving a stain as the mark of the gratification of his passion upon the marble."

There is a similarity in this with the mistake made by a bull which, according to Valerius Maximum, VIII., ch. II., fell in love with a bronze cow, and copulated with the same at Syracuse, being deceived by the perfection of the resemblance.

CHAPTER V

CUNNILINGUES

E have now said enough about the work of Venus performed by the virile member; it remains for us to explain how a sacrifice may be offered to Venus without one. This may be done by means of the tongue or of the clitoris. We have accordingly first to treat of the cunnilingues, those who lick women's privates and then of the tribads.

As it is the office of the *fellator* or *fellatrix* to suck the virile parts, so it is the business of cunnilingues to lick the female. The cunnilingue operates by introducing his tongue into the vulva. Martial (XI., 62) has described his monstrous act very clearly:

"Manneius, husband with his tongue, adulterer with his mouth,—more foul than the mouths of harlots of the Summoenium; whom seeing, as he stood naked, from a window, the filthy procuress closed her brothel; whose middle she had rather kiss than his head. He who of old knew all the channels of the inwards, and could declare with a sure and certain voice, whether 'twas a boy or girl in the mother's belly (be glad, all vulvas, for your part is done), can no longer erect his fornicating tongue. For lo! as he lurks with tongue plunged in the swelling vulva and hears the babes wailing inside their mother, a shocking malady paralyses his greedy mouth,—and now he can no more be either clean or unclean."

By the same paralysis of the tongue Zoilus was struck; Martial, XI., 86:

"An evil star, Zoilus, has struck your tongue of a sudden, even while licking a vulva. Of a surety, Zoilus, you must now use your member."

Bæticus, the castrated priest of Cybelé, against whom Martial has directed *Epigram* III., 81, was a cunnilingue:

"What have you, Bæticus, a priest of Cybelé to do with the female pit? That tongue of yours by rights should lick men's middles. For what was your member amputated with a Samian potsherd, if the woman's parts had so much charm for you? You must have your *head* castrated; true, you are a castrated Gallus in your secret parts, but none the less you violate the rites of Cybelé; you are a man so far as concerns your *mouth.*"

If this passage were in the least doubtful, *Epigram* 77 of the same book might offer difficulties, not otherwise:

"Some latent sickness of your stomach I suspect. Why, I wonder, Bæticus, are you an *eater of filth?*"

In fact the *fellator* as well as the *cunnilingue* may be called eaters of filth, as in the passage of Galen quoted previously, where both of them are called *coprophagi* (dung-eaters). Bæticus however has only to do with the female pit; he is a *cunnilingue,* not a *fellator.* On the contrary, the lewd tongue of Tongilion (III., 84) is that of a *fellator,* not of a *cunnilingue;* for the tongue of a *cunnilingue* plays the part of a lover, being active; while that of a *fellator* acts the part of a prostitute, remaining passive. Sometimes for want of attention the most learned commentators are at fault in elucidating these playful passages. One of the twin brothers, who in our friend of Bilbilis (the poet Martial) (III., 88), are licking different groins, was a *cunnilingue*. The neighbor of Priapus, "by whose fault it is unhappy Landacé swears she can hardly walk, she is so enlarged," is covertly designated as a *cunnilingue* (*Priapeia* LXXVIII.); yet for all that Scioppius maintains he was only a fornicator; but why should we turn away from the proper sense of the word on account of the enlarged aperture? As if the vulva could not be enlarged, or relaxed by the tongue of the *cunnilingue* equally as much as by active cohabitation!

Tiberius Cæsar in his retreat at Capri does not seem to have disdained the voluptuousness of the *cunnilingue*. Blasted by every other kind of abomination, of what else is the Emperor accused in the Atellanian song, mentioned by Suetonius (*Tiberius,* ch. 45), which was so much applauded:

"An old buck licking the vulvas of goats." but this of being a *cunnilingue?* Do you want to see Tiberius employed at his licking?

Plate XXII., in *Monuments de la privée des douze Césars,* represents it.

So also Sextus Clodius, whom Cicero frequently reproaches with the impurity of his mouth and the obscenity of his tongue (*Pro Domo,* chs. 10 and 18; *Pro Coelio,* ch. 32), appears to us to have been a *cunnilingue.* Hence, that hit of Cicero, in his *Pro domo,* ch. 18:

"My good Sextus, allow me to tell you, as you are already a good dialectician, you are also a good licker."

Certainly if he was one, he was bound to lick Clodia, the sister of Publius Clodius (12), the wife of Metellus, the woman that was intimate with all the world. Cicero, *Pro domo,* ch. 31:

"Ask Sextus Clodius as to this, cite him to appear; he is keeping quite in the background. But if you will have him looked for, he will be found near your sister (he is

(12) But Clodia was something more than a sister for Publius Clodius; this would appear from the spirited pleasantry of Cicero, *Pro Coelio,* ch. 13:

"If there had not arisen differences between me and that lady's husband, . . . brother, I would say; I always make that mistake."

addressing Publius Clodius), lurking some-
where with his head low."

Pay attention, pray, to this expression: "the
head low," it will soon re-appear, when we
speak of the Greeks.

The Greeks, in fact, felt no repugnance to
the pleasure in question. *Epigrams* LXXIV.,
LXXV., and LXXVI., in the *Analecta* of
Brunck, vol. III., p. 165, allude to this:

LXXIV.

"Homer taught you to call voice ****; but
who taught you to have the tongue **** (in
a slit)?"

The unknown poet plays upon the ambiguity of the word ****, which is used with
respect to the tongue in an honest sense, when
derived from ****, I speak, but as a vile
usage when derived from ***, a slit.

LXXV.

"Avoid Alpheus' mouth, he loves Are-
thusa's bosom, plunging head-first into the
salty sea."

In this epigram also the poet draws upon
the ambiguity of the words mouth, bosom
(bay), head-first, salt sea, which may refer

to the river Alpheus in Arcadia and to Are-
thusa, a spring near Syracuse, but also to the
mouth of a *cunnilingue,* that goes and plunges
into the vulva of a woman; not to mention
yet another idea connected with this, to
which we shall return presently.

LXXVI.

"Cheilon and **** have the same letters,
and why? It is because Cheilon will lick
things that are like and unlike."

This mockery is addressed to the cunnilingue Cheilon. The epigram tells him that
he has somehow a right of licking, as his
name, composed of the same letters as ****,
announces at once the licker, whether he may
lick the lips of a mouth, similar to his own,
or those of a vulva, which are very dissimilar.

The distich of Meleager upon Phavorinus,
published by Huschkius in his *Analecta crit-
ica* (p. 245), seems to bear upon the same
subject:

"You doubt whether Phavorinus does the
thing. Doubt no more; he told me himself
he did,—*with his own mouth.*"

As Martial uses often very happily the word *narrat* (III., 84), when he speaks of the abuse of the tongue for *fellation,* and Horace the same, so Meleager says **** (he told) of the man, who employs his for licking the vulva.

The following epigram of Ammanius from the *Analecta* of Brunck, vol. II., p. 386, is somewhat more obscure:

"It is not because you suck your pen that I dislike you; 'tis because you do so,—without a pen."

The scholiast imagined by author wanted to upbraid a lazy pupil who passed his time sucking his pen, as do others biting their nails, and to scold him at the same time for sucking without a pen, meaning for being a *cunnilingue.* But it may be taken to refer, and I think with more reason, to a man who is in the habit of putting out his tongue for the obscene act of the *cunnilingue,* and who is so accustomed to it that he puts it out in the ordinary intercourse of life.

This monstrous practice was pushed to such lengths that, it is almost incredible, there were people who, not content to lick vulvas

which were dry, did it when they were humid
with the menses or any other secretion. Aristophanes says of Ariphrades in the *Knights,*
v. 1280-83:

"He is not only lewd; his fancy goes
astray; he pollutes his tongue with shameful
pleasures, licking up in his orgies the abominable dew, fouling his beard and tormenting women's privates."

Tormenting women's privates, licking the
dews, staining the beard, there you have the
man whom humid vulvas do not disgust!
there you have a beard like that of the Ravola
of Juvenal (IX., 4), "when he with beard
all moist was rubbing against the groin of
Rhodopé." However, not to be dogmatic,
it may be admitted that Ravola's moist beard
may have been intended merely the wet hair
of a fornicator's pubis. From the above passage of Aristophanes we may deduce surely
enough that the expression "working with
the tongue," which he also uses, rather am-
biguously, with respect to the same Ariphrades, applies to a *cunnilingue* rather than
to a *fellator, Wasps,* 1847-77:

"Then Ariphrades, the best endowed of all,

of whom his father said once, he never had a teacher, but prompted by nature, of his own free will, learned how to work his tongue, visiting every brothel!"

The same personage re-appears in the *Peace,* 885, where he is described without any circumlocution as imbibing the feminine secretion by way of a sauce:

"And throwing himself on her he will drink up all her juice."

The Greeks, however, had in this kind of voluptuousness a host of imitators amongst the Romans. Mamercus Scaurus is known to us through Seneca (*De Beneficiis,* IV., ch. 31), in this light:

"Did you not know when you appointed Mamercus Scaurus as Consul, that he swallowed the menses of his servant girls by the mouthful? Did he make a secret of it? Did he pretend to be a blameless man?"

Similarly with Natalis, letter LXXXVII.:

"Lately Natalis, that man with a tongue as malicious as it is impure, in whose mouth women used to eject their monthly purgation. . . ."

Both of them were consequently "imbibers

of menses," an appellation which, as we have seen in chapter III, Galen applies to *cunnilingues*.

Now too we can clearly understand the meaning of Nicharchus' epigram against Demonax, vol. III., p. 334 of Brunck's *Analecta*:

"Do not, Demonax, regard all things with downcast head, and do not spoil your tongue with over-gratification; the sow has threatening bristles. You live amongst us, but you sleep in Phœnicia, and though no son of Semelé, you are thigh-reared."

He never looks up, exactly like the Cinede Maternus of Martial, I., 97; he gratifies his tongue, which likes erection; whether the vulva be covered with hair or depilated, he does not mind; during the day he lives in Greece, but sleeps in Phœnicia, because he stains his mouth with the monthly flux, which is, as every one knows, of the Phœnician dye, viz., purplish red (13); like another Bacchus,

---

(13) Gonzalvo of Cordova, according to Aloysia Sigaea (Dialogue VIII.), made similar jokes: "He also, I am sure, in spite of his age, was a great tongue-player (linguist). A pretty girl of some twenty years had to amuse him. When he wanted to put his tongue to her

he draws his nourishment from a thigh (14).
This scarcely needs an explanation. You
can picture the *cunnilingue,* with his mouth
glued between the thighs, at work.

---

juste milieu, he declared he wanted to go to Liguria." He
could play with words upon the same matter, always im-
plying the idea of a humid vulva, saying that he was going
to Phœenicia, or to the Red Sea, or to the Salt Lake;
you now understand what is meant by the Salt Lake or
Salt Sea, into which Alpheus threw himself according to
the epigram in the *Anthology.* Nearly related to this
are the salgamas of Ausonius, of which we shall speak
shortly, and the "onions swimming in putrid brine,"
which the Bæticus of Martial (III., 77) devours. As
it was said of the fellators that they "Phœenicized", because they followed the example set by the Phœenicians, so
probably the same word was applied to the *cunnilingues*
as loving to swim in a certain sea of Phœenician red; and,
in fact, this was the case. Hesychius: "Scylax, an Erotic
posture, like that assumed by Phœenicizers." The Phœenicians assumed a certain posture, called Scylax, or *the dog.*
There could be nothing better for describing the depraved
action of a *cunnilingue* than this canine epithet with regard to the posture taken for irrumating or fellation; dogs
are *cunnilingues* as anybody knows, and have been so ever
since their abominable adventure which their ambassadors
met with (allusion to Phædrus' fable).

(14) Ovid, *Metamorphoses,* III., 308-12:

". . . Mortal woman could not survive the celestial
fire; she was consumed by her spouse's favours. The in-
fant but half formed is torn from the mother's womb, and,
if we may believe the tale, is sown still immature in the
father's thigh, and there completes the period of ges-
tation."

This strange depravity was still in favor in succeeding centuries. Ausonius, in his *Epigrams* CXX, CXXIII, CXXV., CXXVI., CXXVII., and CXXVIII, has bequeathed a very unenviable notoriety to the names of Castor and of Eunus:

Epigram CXX.:

"Castor (15) wanted to lick the middle part of men, but he could not persuade any one to go with him; however the *fellator* did not miss his treat; he went and licked his own wife's privates."

Epigram CXXIII, entitled *In Eunum liguritorem.*—On Eunus the Licker:

"Eunus, why do you pay court to Phyllis, the perfume seller? Men say your tongue knows her parts, but not your member! Mind you make no mistakes in the names of her scents and perfumes, and that Seplasia's atmosphere play you no tricks; think not costus and cysthus have the same odor,—that sardines and nard exhale the same savor.

---

(15) This Castor is perhaps the same who, according to the statement of Ausonius (Epigram *in Professoribus Burdegalensibus,* XXII., 7) had published a book with the title *Cunctis de Regibus ambiguis.*

Poor Eunus! the things that he tastes and smells are very different; his mouth and his nose have tastes widely dissimilar!"

He says mockingly: think not the sundry wares in the shop of Phyllis your little perfume seller of Capua (Seplasia is in fact a street of the town of Capua, where perfumes were sold), are all of the same odor and savor. The costus (16) does not smell like the cysthus (17), the nard (18) has a different flavor from the sardines,—a sort of little fish preserved in salt. By this salty condiment Ausonius means to imply precisely the same as the author of the Greek epigram signifies, when he speaks of the Salt Sea, and which he himself has called salgama, meaning the secretion of the humid vulva. But Eunus shows no discrimination between what he licks and what he smells; the two have

(16)   Pliny, *Nat. Hist.,* XII, ch. 12: "The Costus-root has a burning taste and an exquisite smell; its berries are otherwise useless."

(17)   The Cysthus, Greek **** is the private parts of a woman.   Aristophanes, *Lysistrata,* v. 1160: "And a more beautiful cysthus I never saw."

(18)   Pliny *Nat. Hist.,* XII., ch. 12: "The leaves of the nard must be considered more minutely, for they are a principal ingredient in perfumery."

nothing in common. He inhales perfumes which smell beautifully, and licks the vulva, which smells abominably. His nose obeys one law, his tongue another.

Epigram CXXV, directed against the same Eunus:

"The salgamas are no balmy odors; give place, all other perfumes. I would rather not smell at all, either good or bad."

Here again the poet plays with the words. The perfumes which Phyllis sells he calls balms, and salgamas those which her vulva exhales. Properly speaking, salgamas are roots and greens, which are preserved in salt for winter use, and the odor of which is not pleasant to every one's nose. His saying that he would rather smell nothing at all than smell something bad is borrowed from Martial VI., epigr. 55, against Coracinus, who was a *cunnilingue*:

"Rather than smell bad scents I would not smell at all."

Epigram CXXVI:

"Lais, Eros and Itys, Chiron and Eros, Itys once again,—if you write the names, and take the initial letters, they make a word,

and that word is what you do, Eunus. What
that word is and means, decency lets me not
say in plain Latin."

The initial letters of the six Greek names
form the word ****, he licks. The phallic
poet (*Priapeia* LXVII) plays in the same
way upon the word *paedicare* (to pedicate):

"Take the first syllable of *P*enelopé; add
to it the first of *D*ido; then to the first of
*C*anis append the first of *R*emus: what they
make, I will do to you, thief, if I catch you
in my garden. This is the penalty your crime
will meet."

Ausonius plays on the words *doing* and
making. The initials of the Greek words
make a word he cannot say in Latin,—it is
too indecent. Yet Eunus has no hesitation
in *doing* it,—putting it in action.

Epigram CXXVII:

"Eunus, when you lick the groins of your
wife, she being with child; 'tis because you
would be betimes in *teaching the tongues*
to your babes yet unborn."

You seem, he says, to send out your tongue
to meet your unborn children, and fulfilling
your duty as a Grammarian, to teach them

lessons of tongue, and the interpretation of obscure terms (19). The Manneius of Martial, whom we have spoken of above, was also in the habit of licking pregnant women's privates.

Epigram CXXVIII., entitled *On the same Eunus, the Learned Licker*:

"Eunus, the little Syrian pedagogue, licker of privates, Opican doctor ('tis Phyllis he owes his knowledge to), beholds the feminine engine in fourfold different fashions: Opening it triangularly, he makes it the letter Delta ($\triangle$); seeing the pair of folds side by side along the valley of the thighs with the

---

(19) "Quintilian, *Instit. orat.*, I, ch. 1: "He can learn the interpretation of the occult languages, what the Greeks call ****** Alcuin, *Grammatica*, p. 2086, in Putschius' *Collection*: *Glossa* is the interpretation of a verb or a noun; e.g. *catus* is the same thing as *doctus.*" On this occasion it may be permitted to the Director of the Court-Library at Coburg to state, that this library contains a remarkable copy of the collection of Putschius, by the hand of John Scheffer, who died at Upsala in 1679, beginning thus: "The notes to be found in this volume, on the margin of books IV and V, of Priscian, have been made after a very ancient and most beautifully written manuscript, in which a number of traces of primitive Latin orthography are found, as for instance: *dirivare* for *derivare, peneultimus* and *antepeneultimus* for *penultimus* and *antepenultimus, Oratius* for *Horatius,* etc."

line in the middle where the slit of the vagina opens, he says it is a Psi (*) ; in fact its shape is triple-cloven then. Then when he has put his tongue in, it is a Lambda (*), and he makes out therein the true design of a Phi (*). Why! ignoramus, do you think you see a Rho (P.) written, where merely a long Iota (I.) should be put? Contemptible doctor, foul pedant, you deserve the Tau (T.) yourself; the crossed Theta (O.) should by rights be put against your name."

Ausonius calls Eunus an Opican, because these filthy practices were, according to Festus, most common among the Osci or Opici. He then indulges in a series of jests, or rather represents Eunus as doing so, on the shape of the female organ (20). He says it seems

(20) As we are on the subject of the shape of the female organ, it will not be amiss to enumerate in this place all the various names by which it was known in Latin; the greater part of them we have gathered from the treasure-house of Aloysia Sigaea: "The field, the ring, the furrow, the cavern, the clitoris, the conch-shell, the cunnus, the little boat, the cysthus, the pit, the garden, the between-thighs, the barque, the swine, the wicket, the slit, the precipice, the hole, the trench, the sheath, the virginal, the vulva. And what should hinder us from giving at the time time the names of the virile member: The armature of the belly, the catapult, the tail, the stem,

to him either quadrangular, or triangular, in the latter case corresponding to the Greek Δ (similarly Aristophanes called it a Delta, —"their delta plucked clean of hair," *Lysistrata,* 151), and also likens it to the letter **, owing to the folds which surround the vulva on either side (21), and form the outer lips, the lane in the middle being the opening of the vulva, and so together form the trifid letter **; in the *Technopaegnium,* 140, he calls it a three-pronged fork, the slit being the middle and the lips the outer prongs. Then he says that Eunus is a Lambda when he is licking, on account of the first letter of

---

the parcel, the column, the pole, the lance with balls, the amulet, the pike, the groin, the hanger, the mentula, the mutinus, the muto, the nerve, the virile sign, the stake, the peculia, the penis, the stopper, the phallus, the javelin, the tree, the obelisk, the shaft, the spectre, the seminal member, the awl, the bull, the dart, the balista, the beam, the thyrsus, the vessel, the little vessel, the vein, the private, the verpa and verpus, the verge, the ploughshare. Here you have more than enough.

(21) *Altrinsecus,* in Ausonius, is equivalent to *utrinsecus,* meaning, from either side. Lactantius employs that word in *De Opificio Dei,* ch. 8: "It is incredible how the fact of their being double (the ears) adds to their beauty, as much on account of the symmetry thus produced, as because the sounds which arise on all sides, can more easily be received on both sides (altrinsecus)."

the word **** All this is clear enough, and I do not understand how the very learned Vinet can complain of its obscurity. Neither has it given me much trouble to make out what Ausonius means by the letters Rho and Iota. The solution seems to me to be as follows: "Do not tell us, Eunus, that your pike in action resembles the letter P of the Greeks, a letter which evidently looks like a lance with balls; in your amorous diversions you use no other lance than your tongue, which, as you will not deny, looks more like a javelin without balls, something like the letter Iota; you cannot deceive me, who well know that you would rather be taken for a fornicator than for a *cunnilingue,* like that Gargilius, of whom Martial, III, 96, says:

"You do not enter, only lick my mistress; yet you boast yourself adulterer and copulator!"

Lastly and finally by the Tau he threatens his man with the gallows, and by the Theta with death. Of this there can be little doubt; it is a proved fact that the letter Theta, the initial of the word ****, signified

with the Greeks condemnation to death (22).
With regard to Tau, there is room for doubt;
instead of Tau some of the copies of Ausonius give 8, and although this sign may, according to Scaliger, very well signify the
rope for hanging, the difficulty I feel is this,
that a composite letter, a small letter, an ab-
breviation of doubtful antiquity, thus placed
amongst simple, capital, unabbreviated letters seems to come in very inappropriately.
It may be that Ausonius originally wrote
****; then * having been left out by an in-
advertence of the copyist, the ** might easily
have been turned into **. The Tau, as the
reader will see at once, represents a gallows.
Tertullian, *Adversus Maricionem*: "This letter Tau of the Greeks is with us the T, a sort
of cross."

As was the case with irrumation, so with
even more reason the licking of women's
privates was particularly adopted by old men,
whose tool will not raise its head (23).

---

(22) Persius, VI, 13: "And you may mark the crime
with a black Theta." See also Martial, VII, 36.

(23) I say it was adopted by them particularly; that
there were also young men, who by a singular depravity

Aloysia Sigaea, Dialogue VII, says: "He (Gonzalvo of Cordova), was likewise a mighty *cunnilingue* by reason of his great age."

"Why does Blatara lick? because he cannot manage otherwise."

The same author, VI, 26:

"Lotades has lost the power of stiffening; so licks."

And again, XII, 88:

"Thirty young boys you have at command, and as many girls; yet you have only one member, and that will not rise. What then will you do?"

Lick, no doubt, as we are told Linus did, in Epig. XI, 25:

"This too frisky mentula, Linus, so well known to girls in plenty, will longer stand; so mind your tongue."

Sextillus (Martial II, 28), was in all probability also a *cunnilingue*:

"Have your laugh at those, Sextillus, that

---

licked the vulvas they might have entered legitimately, Martial tells us, XI, 86:

"An evil star, Zoilus, has struck your tongue of a sudden, even while licking a vulva. Of a surety, Zoilus, you must now use your member."

call you cinede, and show them your middle
finger (24). You are not, Sextillus, a pedicon nor yet a fornicator, nor does Vetustilla's
burning mouth tempt you.—You are none of
these, I allow, Sextillus; then what are you?
I know not, but remember! there are two
sorts yet."

Two sorts are still left for Sextillus, to
suck the virile member and to lick the vulva,
while he is neither a fornicator, nor a cinede,
nor a pedicon, nor an irrumator. Which
did he choose to be? This we are not told.
Eunuchs, just as impotent as aged men, adopt

---

(24) When the middle-finger is pointing, the other
fingers are turned inside, representing thus a mentula
with its accessories; for which reason it was thus pointedly
shown to Cinedes (the Greeks expressed this in a single
word: ******), either by way of invitation or to tease
them. Martial, I, 93: "Cestus has often complained
to me, Mamurianus, that you tease him with your finger."
It was also pointed at people held in contempt. The same
author, VI, 70:

"He points with the finger and that the impudent
finger" (that is Martianus, who is never ill, does to the
doctors). Thence this unlucky finger had the epithet "infamous." Persius says without any obscene afterthought,
II, 33: "The grandmother cleanses the babe with the
infamous (middle) finger."

the practice for the same reason (25). Gregory Nazianzen says in his funeral sermon on Basil the Great:

---

(25) Nevertheless, Eunuchs who have been deprived of their testicles, but not of their mentula, are by no means wanting in lubricity: they can do the business without any danger for a woman, inasmuch as they cannot generate children. The Roman matrons were well aware of the fact: Martial, VI., 67:

"You ask me, Pannicus, why Gallia keeps so many Eunuchs; she loves to be enjoyed, but wants no children."

Juvenal, VI, 365-67:

"There are women who like feeble eunuchs, and kisses that are ever harmless, and the absence, nay! the impossibility, of a beard, for they need use no abortive."

St. Jerome, in the *Life of Hilarion*: "A steward with curled locks, castrated for the sake of longer pleasure and perfect safety. . . ." To make more sure of their enjoyment, experienced dames did not allow the testicles of the Eunuchs to be cut off until the member had attained full proportions, apprehensive that it might remain puny and inactive if the operation were made earlier. They wanted their Eunuchs well furnished, capable of challenging Priapus himself. By such they liked to be worked, being sure of not becoming enceinte. Juvenal, VI., 367-77:

"With those however is love's pleasure most exquisite, whose testicles, when they are lusty and fully matured, are delivered to the surgeons, the pubis being already black with hair. The organs are spared till they are full and ready; then at last, when they have reached two pounds in weight, Heliodorus cuts them, to the prejudice of the barber. The observed of all observers, stared at by all, see him enter the baths and challenge the god

"They of the gynaeceum, those men, who amongst women are men, and amongst men women; who have nothing virile about them but their impiety; those that cannot give themselves up to voluptuousness in the natural way, have recourse to their tongue as their only alternative."

The *cunnilingues* exhaled an evil smell from the mouth, and their kisses were as much shunned as those of *fellators*. Martial, XII., 87:

"You say the mouths of pedicons smell badly; if this is true, Fabullus, as you say, tell me! what think you of the breath of *cunnilingues?*"

And the same, XII., 59:

"The neighbors kiss you every one, from the bearded cowherd, whose kisses have flavor of the he-goat, down to the *fellator* and the *cunnilingue* fresh from his business."

Cunnilingues and *fellators* are compared to

---

of vineyard and garden, castrated thus by his lady's order. He may sleep now with his mistress; still beware, Josthumus, how you trust him with your Bromius, now fully developed and ready for the razor."

he-goats by Catullus (XXXVII.), on account of their fetid breath:

"Think you you alone have members, that you alone are entitled to satisfy women, and may consider all other men he-goats?"

Do not suppose for a moment that Catullus is speaking here of castrated he-goats, which would be against the sense of the word, one invariably used to designate entire he-goats. The sense is the same, but got at in another way. He says: "Do you believe that you alone have members fit to do the girls' business? that all the others betray by their goatish breath their vile trade as *cunnilingues* or *fellators,* and consequently the inertness of their mentulas, their feebleness, their inability for erection? You will better appreciate the sting of Atellane verse respecting Tiberius Cæsar: "An old buck licking the she-goats' parts."

It was thought better to be taken for a fornicator than for a *cunnilingue;* in the first place, because your friends would not kiss you; Martial, VII., 94:

"I had rather confront a hundred *cunnilingues.*"

Suetonius, *De Illustribus Grammaticis,* ch. 23:

"He (Remmius Palaemon) was passionately fond of women, so much so as to prostitute his mouth to please them, and it is said that he was one day rebuked in the following way by a man who in the throng could not contrive to avoid one of his kisses: "Master," he said, "if you see a man in a hurry to get away, will you lick him off?"

In the second place for fear of scaring away your guests. Aristophanes says of Ariphrades, in the *Knights,* 1285, 86:

"Whoever does not execrate that man, may he never drink from the same cup with us"— lastly, for fear of letting it be plainly known how shrunken one was, and how miserable one's member. Martial, III, 96:

"You lick my mistress, but you do not enter her; yet you boast yourself adulterer and copulator!"

Hence the *cunnilingues* took no less care than the *fellators* to hide the fetidness of their breath by means of essences and perfumes, Martial VI, 55:

Always scented with cassia and cinnamon,

and your skin darkened with perfumes from the Phoenix' nest, you reek of the leaden jars of Nicerotus' shop. You mock at us, Coracinus, because we are unscented. Rather than smell sweet like you, I'd not smell at all."

To remove every doubt as to Coracinus being a *fellator* or a *cunnilingue,* we will quote *Epigr.* IV, 43, where he is expressly called a *cunnilingue:*

"I did not say you were a cinede, Coracinus; I am not so rash and reckless. What I did say in a light, insignificant matter, one perfectly well known, that you will not deny yourself,—I said, Coracinus, you were a *cunnilingue."*

It was believed that Venus revenged injuries done to herself or to hers, not only by condemning the guilty to submit to be the passive party, but by turning them into *cunnilingues.* Hence the pathic tastes of Philoctetes:

"With which the destitution of Lemnos inspired the heir of Heracles."

To use the very words of Ausonius, *Epigr.* LXXI; and by inflicting these tastes Venus

is said to have avenged the wounds of Paris,
Martial, II, 84:

"The sons of Poeas was effeminate and
prone to man-love; thus they say did Venus
avenge Paris' wounds."

In the same epigram Martial rallies Sertorius on being cunnilingue, giving as a possible reason his having killed Eryx, the son
of Venus:

"Why does Sicilian Sertorius lick women's
privates; because, Rufus, it would seem it
was he killed Eryx."

Cunnilingues appear to have been generally pale-faced; it is for medical men to say
why. This may help you to discern the
salt in Martial's epigram on Charinus, I, 78:

"Charinus is well and strong, and still he
is pale;

Charinus drinks with moderation, and still
he is pale;

Charinus digests well, and still he is pale;

Charinus loves the open air and sun, and
still he is pale;

Charinus dyes his skin, and still he is pale;

Charinus licks a woman's privates, and
still pale is he."

That is to say, amongst the causes that should prevent paleness the one last enumerated is the veritable cause of his paleness. *Fellators* would also seem to have had pale faces, Catullus, LXXX:

"How is it, Gellius, that those rosy lips of yours grow whiter than the winter's snow, when at morn you leave your house, and the eighth hour calls you from your long-protracted soft repose? I know not what to think. Can it be true what rumor whispers, that you devour the middle parts of men? This at any rate is evidenced by wretched Virro's sunken flanks and your own lips masked with the milky juice sucked from him."

The withered flanks are those of Virro, the *irrumator,* the lips those of Gellius; the passage is somewhat ambiguous, and only thus to be explained. One Virro, accustomed to take the passive part, has been already mentioned by us, in quoting Juvenal, IX, 35. I do not know whether it is the same:

"Though Virro has caught sight of you all naked, and the foam has come to his lips."

Pathics, too, no less than *fellators*, appear to have pallid faces. Juvenal, II, 50:

"Hispo submits to young men; he is pale with either kind of infamy."

He served as *patient* to young men, and was moreover a *fellator*, as is shown by the difference which the poet institutes between him and women, who do not lick each other's secret parts:

"Taedia does not lick Cluvia, nor Flora Catulla."

Women, in fact, are rarely *cunnilingues*, although there *are* examples. Martial only mentions one woman as belonging to that category; we shall come across her again in the next chapter.

CHAPTER VI

OF TRIBADS

THE tribads, also called frictionists (26) from the Greek ****, I rub, are women, with whom that part of the genital apparatus which is called the clitoris, attains such proportions, that they can use it as a mentula, either for fornication or pedication. The clitoris (27), which is a very sensitive caruncle (a small

(26) They were also called hetairistriae:—Hesychius: "Hetairistriae tribads"—and likewise dietairistriae, according to the same author: "Dietairistriae, women who go after prostitutes (hetairae) for carnal intercourse, just as men do; same as tribads."

(27) Aloysia Sigaea, Dialogue III.: "But I forgot (Tullia speaking) to tell you of the clitoris. This is a membranous body, situated at the bottom of the pubis, and representing in a reduced form the virile verge. As is the case with the verge, the amorous desire excites it to erection, and in certain women of an ardent temperament it inflames them with pruriency to such a degree that by the mere caressing of it with the hand they very often discharge their fluid without the help of a rider at all."

fleshy cone), capable of movement and re-
sembling the verge, gets into erection with
all women, not only during the coitus, the
delights of which it is said to enhance im-
mensely by increased titillation, but also in
consequence of mere amorous longing; with
tribads, either by a freak of nature or in consequence of frequent use, it attains immoderate dimensions (28). The tribad can get

---

(28) If that woman whom Plater saw, according to
Venette in his *Tableau de l'amour conjugal,* vol. I., ch. 1,
3, was not a tribad, she might well have been one; her
clitoris, which with other women attains in its utmost
erection the length of the half of the little finger or there-
abouts, was as long as the neck of a goose. Is it surprising that women furnished with such an implement
should wish to get rid of it? Amputation is however
dangerous. Plater did not venture to finish an amputation which he had commenced, and Rodohamides, an
Egyptian physician of the XIth century, had not courage
to even undertake one, although commanded by a queen
to perform the operation (Venette, IV., 2). Those whom
Adramytes, the king of the Lydians, order to castrate
women, were they more courageous? Athenæus, XII.,
2: "Xanthus states in the second book of his Lydiacs, that
Adramytes, king of the Lydians, was the first to have
women castrated and employ them as eunuchs." However that may be, these female eunuchs have very much
exercised the commentators. Some suppose that straps
and buckles did in their case the same service as the chas-
tity-belts, which, it is said, Spaniards and Italians to this
day compel their wives to wear if they think they have

it in erection, enter a vulva or anus, enjoy a
delicious voluptuousness, and procure if not

---

reason to be jealous: others believe that it was a question
of suture, as is the case with the natives of Angola and
the Congo, who stitch the vulvas of young girls for the
protection of their maidenheads; but I believe that nobody
knows anything certain in this respect. Nor does it appear that these women had to submit to an operation,
which is certainly practised upon the young girls by the
Arabs, Copts, Ethiopians, in some parts of Persia and
Nigritia, and which consists in cutting off the prepuce of
the clitoris; this is proved by abundant evidence, and reported in the Encyclopedia of Ersch and Gruber under
the word: "Beschneidung" (Circumcision); how indeed
could Athenæus describe as *Eunuchize* that which is calculated to increase the fecundity of women. I thought
first that these women were tribads changed into eunuchs
by the removal of their immoderately large clitoris; I am
now inclined to believe that the king caused that to be
done to these women, which according to Aristotle, *Nat.
Hist.* IX., 50, was done to sows: "Sows are castrated,
so that they shall no longer desire the coitus and get
quickly fattened. They are castrated, suspended by their
hind legs, after fasting two days, by an incision in that
place where with a man the testicles are situated, in fact in
the female matrix." Pliny, *Nat. Hist.*, VIII., 51: "Sows
are castrated in the same way as female camels, after a
fast of two days, suspended by their hind legs, by an incision in the vulva; they thus fatten much quicker."
Columella, VII., IX. 5: "Sows are also castrated by incision in the vulva; the wounds cicatrics, and they cannot
conceive any more." This practice has by no means disappeared; Schneider notes it in the passage of Columella;
sows, cows, mares, sheep, are still castrated by excising
their ovarium. Why should we not believe that Adramy-

a complete realization of cohabitation, at least something very near to it, to the woman who plays the passive part. What more is there to say? She plays the man's part with the omission of the ejaculation of the semen, not that this sort of coitus is an altogether dry affair, as women are in the habit of emitting their liquid during the joys of love (29).

tes wanted the same process to be applied to the fair sex, in order to make women sterile? However the ancient Egyptians, who (see Strabo, book XVII., p. 824) undoubtedly circumcized themselves, and also their women, appear to me to have had in view not so much ovariotomy as the circumcision of the prepuce of the clitoris, a practice still in use with them, as stated above; cutting the female parts being thus something like circumcision, it is to be assumed that a similar operation was intended rather than any other one.

(29) Let us consult again Aloysia Sigæa, Dialogue III.: "It has happened sometimes to myself (Tullia), when Callias tries on me his lubricities, when he tickles me and excites me. Then I sometimes water his too libertine hands with an abundant dew from my pleasure grounds. And that gives him an opportunity for letting off a whole sheaf of sarcasms and jokes. But what can I do? I begin to laugh, and so does he; I tell him he is too impudent, he tells me I am too lewd; we call each other names right and left, and in the midst of our mutual recrimination he will throw himself upon me, turn me on my back, and force me to submit to his assault, saying he will give me his dewdrops for those he has

This depravity of voluptuousness, whether
caused by the warmth of the climate, or by a
peculiarity of the soil or waters, or other reasons unknown to us, was especially common
with the women of Lesbos; this is attested by
all the old writers. Lucian, in his "Dialogues of Courtezans," No. V. (Works, vol.

---

drawn from me, so that I may not be a loser." Further
on, Dial., IV.: "Callias, pressing me more closely to him,
buried his weapon deeper into my belly, almost as though
he were trying to get himself in altogether. Soon a delicious stream spirted into me, and at the same time I
felt my liquid boiling over, causing me such delight that
I forgot all reticence, and myself excited Callias more
and more, pressing him against me and begging him to
quicken his pace. Thus we expired both together with
our muscles relaxing at one and the same instant." You
will understand by this the meaning of the epigram to
Sosipator in the *Analecta* of Brunck, I., p. 504:
"Until the white liquor ran over with both of them,
and Doras unwound her wearied limbs."
Reiske thought the "white liquor" in this passage meant
drops of perspiration. Nonsense! it means the virus secreted by both sexes, and liberated in the last spasms of
lust. Aloysia Sigæa, Dialogue IV.: "As I finished speaking" (it is still Tullia that speaks), "he got upon me,
and collecting all his strength he pushed the arrow into
me, he filled my womb with his fecundating dew, and I
also shed the rivulet of white liquid. Incapable of enduring any longer so intense a voluptuous feeling, we sank
back exhausted in each other's arms." We have quoted
besides on different occasions extracts from the rich treasures of Aloysia Sigæa, on this subject.

VII, p. 349.) : "This is one of those tribads, as they are to be found in Lesbos, who will have nothing to do with men, and do the men's business with women." If such things were an every day occurrence with the Lesbian women, we must believe that they were pushed to them by natural instigation (30), and to allay an intolerable pruriency. Who has not heard of that most celebrated queen of all tribads, Sappho, herself a Lesbian? Some authors, Maximum of Tyre the first among them, have with the best intention tried to exonerate her from his infamous vice; but hear her in Ovid (and he represents the Ancients in sentiment and feeling), repudiating her would be opologists, *Heroides,* XV, 15-20:

"Neither the maidens of Pyrrha, nor those of Methymna (31), nor all the host of Les-

---

(30) Women, whose clitoris is too prominent, are thus prevented from having intercourse with men, so that when they are seized with amorous designs they cannot well find any other way of satisfying their desires than by playing tribadism. (Venette IV., ii, 4.)

(31) Pyrrha and Methymna are towns in Lesbos. Pomponius Mela, II, 7: "In the Troad is Lesbos, and in Lesbos there were formerly five cities, viz.: Antissa, Pyrrha, Eresos, Methymna, Mytilene.

bian beauties please me. Vile to me seems
Anactoria, vile the fair Cydno, Atthis is no
more so dear to my eyes as once she was, nor
yet a hundred others I loved not innocently
(32). Villian! yours is now what belonged
to many women. . . ."
and verse 201:

"Lesbian women, beloved, who made me
infamous!"

Sappho speaks first in general of those that
have submitted to her caresses, the maidens
of Pyrrha and Methymna; then she mentions
by name Anactoria, Cydno and Atthis,—to
whom Suidas adds Telesippa and Megara:

"Her favorites, whom she loved well, were
three in number, Atthis, Telesippa, Megara,
and for those she burnt in impure passion."

These passages from the Ancients are clear

---

(32) Not innocently, or rather, "not without crime";
some read "which I loved not without crime" others,
"which I loved here without crime," but the difference
is not great. If you prefer "which I loved here," the
excuse itself is a confession. All we want is the admission
that the tribad-tastes of Sappho are no modern invention,
but originated, how we know not, and prevailed in very
early times. The love of woman for woman was never
known under any other name than the notorious one of
tribadism.

enough, and do not admit of any doubt; they even assist us in explaining other sentences, which otherwise seem obscure or ambiguous; for instance the "masculine Sappho" of Horace (*Epistles* I, XIX, 28); "making plaint against the maids of her country" (*Odes* II, XIII, 25); also Ovid, *Art of Love,* III, 331.

"Sappho should be well known, too; what more wanton than she?" *Tristia,* II, 363:

"What was the lore Lesbian Sappho taught, but to love maids?"
and Martial, VII, 68 (33).

"Sappho, the amorous, praised our poetess; the latter was more pure, the former not more perfect in art."

Lucian's witty and licentious pen has made famous another tribad, Megilla, in the above quoted Dialogue. This Dialogue is not outrageously obscene, for it breaks off just at the moment when things would have had to be said very plainly; nevertheless, the virginal modesty of our Wieland has not dared to translate it into German. The philosopher

---

(33) See whether it is with good reason or no that the succeeding epigram, no. 69, calls Philaenis the tribad of tribads.

of Samosata brings Leaena upon the scene,
and makes her disclose by what artifices Megilla gained her consent. Leana asks Megilla:

"Are you then made like a man, and do
with Demonassa (whom Megilla used after
the manner of tribads), as men do? I have
not got exactly all that, my Leaena," answers
Megilla, "but I am not entirely without it.
However, you will see me at work, and in a
very pleasant manner. I have been born like
all of you, but I have the tastes, the desires
and something else of a man. Let me do it
to you, if you do not believe me, and you
will see that I have everything that men have.
Give me leave to work you, and you will
see." Leaena confesses that she at last consented, moved by her solicitations and promises, and no doubt also by the novelty of
the thing. "I let her have her way," she
says, "yielding to her entreaties, seconded by
a magnificent necklet and a robe of fine linen.
I took her in my arms like a man; she went
to work caressing me, panting with excitement and evidently experiencing the extreme
of pleasure." Clonarion asks her inquisitive-

ly: "But what did she do to you Leaena, and how did she manage?" But Leaena eludes the question. "Do not ask me anything more; these are nasty doings; by Urania, I shall not breathe a word more!" she answers, to the great regret of the reader, who would like to penetrate further this mystery.

Amongst the tribads is still to be named Philaenis, the same, no doubt, who according to Lucian (*Amores,* ch. 28—Works vol. V, p. 88), wrote about erotic postures: "Let our women's apartments be filled by women like Philaenis, dishonored by androgynic (34) loves!—Sophoclidisca in Plautus, to whom Paegnion says: "Do not caress me, subagitatrix!" (*Persa,* act II., 41);—and Folia of Ariminum, who according to Horace (*Epodes,* V, 41) was "of masculine lubricity." However writers as a rule touch upon these points more lightly than is agreeable to the curiosity of the reader. For the same reason the too great reserve of Seneca (*Controversia,* II) is to be regretted, where he says at the end:

(34) To make yourselves quite sure about what the author means by androgynic loves, look at the passage

"Hybreas having to plead in favor of a man who had surprised and killed a tribad, described the grief of the husband; on such a subject one must not ask for a too particular investigation."

Much more complete, full and explicit is our good friend of Bilbilis (Martial). Hear him! he is disclosing the tribadic doings of Balba, so clearly that it could not be done better; I, 91:

"As no one, Bassa, ever saw you go with men; as rumor never assigned you a lover, as every office about you was fulfilled by

---

as a whole: "Come, you man of the new age, you lawgiver of unknown amours, if you open out new ways to the lubricity of men, you may grant to the women equal license. Let them cohabit together as the men do; let woman lie with woman, and simulate with their lascivious organs conjunctions, sterile though they be, as man lies with man! Let the word one hears so very rarely, and which I am ashamed to pronounce, let the lubricity of our tribads triumph without blushing." Observe in the first place how tribads were seldom spoken of, and that they kept themselves in the dark; in the second place how the immoderate clitoris of the tribad is said to simulate lascivious organs in conjunction. Seneca, *Controversia Secunda,* in a similar sense, calls such a monstrosity *****, an *artificial man;* lastly the epithet "sterile" is applied to the clitoris, and points to the dry unproductiveness of the tribadic coitus.

a troop of women, no man ever coming nigh you, you seemed to us, I admit, a very Lucretia. But, oh! shame on you, Bassa, you were a fornicator all the time! You dare to conjoin the private parts of two women together, and your monstrous organ of love feigns the absent male. You have contrived a miracle to match the Thebian riddle: that where no man is, there adultery should be!"

Surely it is clear enough what Bassa did, in conjoining the privates of two women together. By no means! There are expounders, and very good ones, too, who have quite misunderstood this very easy passage, and have imagined that Bassa misused women by introducing into their vagina a leathern contrivance, an olisbos, a *godemiche;* we shall speak at the end of this chapter of this kind of pleasure, but it was quite unknown to Bassa, who simulated the man in her own person.

Nothing could be more monstrous than the libertine passion of Philaenis; she did not content herself with introducing her stiff clitoris in the vulva of tribads, Martial, VII, 69:

"Tribad of tribads, you, Philaenis, you are well justified in calling her your mistress whom you work;" or in those of other young girls, and to get a dozen of them under her in a day; but she even pedicated boys; Martial, VII, 67:

"Philaenis the tribad pedicates boys (35), and stiffer than a man in one day works eleven girls."

In order to leave nothing untasted in the way of virile lusts she was also a *cunnilingue;* same epigram, at the end:

"After all that, when she is in good feather, —she does not suck, that is too feminine; she devours right out girls' middle parts. May all the gods confound you, Philaenis, who think it manly work to lick the vulva."

---

(35) Instead of "pedicating boys," Martial might have said, if the metre had allowed it, "entering boys." Seneca's expression (Letter XCV), *viros ineunt,"* which was a source of great trouble to the great Justus Lipsius, signifies nothing else: "The women will contest for the crown of lubricity with the men. May the gods confound them! one of their refined lubricities reverses the laws of Nature: they have connection with men!" There you have in plain words the turpitude which Justus Lipsius considered worthy of the infernal regions; tribads pedicating.

Philaenis, when overmuch in rut, caused herself also to be served by *cunnilingues;* this is clear enough from Martial, IX, 41:

"When Diodorus, wanting the Tarpeian crowns, left Pharos behind and sailed for Rome, Philaenis vowed that to celebrate her mate's return an innocent maid should lick her, such a one as the chaste Sabine women still cherish."

She vowed if her husband returned to have her vulva licked by a young girl, well-known for her innocence and chastity; to have it done by prostitutes was for Philaenis nothing new; she wanted on that occasion to experiment with a virgin, exactly like men, who always want something new and strange to spur their lust. How rare it was for women to use other women for that purpose appears from Juvenal II, 47-49:

". . . . There will no other instance be found so abominable in our sex; Taedia does not lick Cluvia, nor Flora Catulla."

But what could you find stronger, more energetic and plainer to enlighten the reader completely on this subject than the following verses in *Satire* VI, 308-333, where Juvenal's ire against the tribadic orgies in Rome breaks out in words of fire?

"At night they stop their litters here, make water here, and flood with long syphons the Goddess' statue, and ride turn and turn about and go through the motions under the eye of the conscious moon; then they make for home. When the morning light returns, you walk through your wife's piss, to visit your great friends. Known are the secret rites of the *Bona Dea,* when the flute excite their wanton loins, when drunk with music and with wine they rush along, whirling their locks and howling, these Maenads of Priapus! How they yearn for instant copulation! how their voice trembles with passionate longing! what floods of old wine gush down their dripping thighs! A prize is offered, and Laufeia challenges the brothel-master's girls, and wins the first place for nimble hips; while herself is mad for the pleasure Medullina's artful movements give her. Amongst these dames merit carries off the palm from noble blood. There nothing must be feigned, all must be done in very truth and deed,—enough to set on fire, however chilled with age, Laomedon's son and old Nestor with his rupture! Then is seen mere lust that will brook not a moment's more delay, women in her bare brutality, while from every corner of the subterranean hall rises the reiterated cry: "The hour is come, admit the men." Is the lover asleep? she bids the first young man to hand snatch up his hood and come at once. Is none to be found? resort is had to slaves. No hope of slaves? a water-carrier will be hired to come. If he comes not, and men there are none, she will not wait an instant more but get an ass to mount her from behind."

The tribadic orgies were divided into two kinds; in one of them the Roman dames, giving free course to their lust, defiled the altar of chastity; in the other they celebrated the mysteries of the *Bona Dea*. You see in the first place the tribads go at night in litters to the altar of chastity, there pass their water (36) against the statue of the Goddess,

---

(36) When women are in rut they pass their water, nature wills it so, Juvenal VI, 63-65: "Let lewd Bathyllus dance the pantomine of Leda" (representing Leda receiving Jupiter in a dance with wanton gestures":

and having perhaps spirted their urine up to her face (37) they at all events wet the area all about, (their husbands walking right through it in the morning, when they go to see their patrons), and then they ride or allow themselves to be ridden alternately;

"Tuscia cannot command her bladder, Appula is sighing as if in amorous trance. . . ."

The same XI, 166-168:

"The other sex however feels more pleasure, is much sooner fired, and lets the water off, excited through eyes and ears."

(What Juvenal says here as to this greater enjoyment on the part of the opposite sex is connected with his general opinion that women experience more pleasure in Love than men do. So his words in VI, 254: For how insignificant is our pleasure!" Tiresias, called upon to arbitrate on this point in Lucian (*Amores,* p. 85), declared women's enjoyment to be double that of men: "Unless indeed we are to agree with Tiresias' arbitrement, that the woman's pleasure is twice that of the man").

Martial XI, 17:

"How often will your rigid nerve lift up your tunic, though you be as stern as Curius or Fabricius! You too have to read our pages, be they ever so lascivious, young maiden, though you come from Padua."

(37) There is some ambiguity about the "long syphons." They are rivulets of urine passed near the statue, or perhaps Juvenal means, to use the expression of Grangé, "Urine spirted right up into the Goddess' face, which may be done by impudent women compressing with the hands their parts, and thus retaining for some time

here we have more than on Philaenis, tribad of tribads! Other ladies go to celebrate the mysteries of the *Bona Dea,* well known to the public since the adventures of Clodius (38). You observe them rousing themselves with the sounds of flutes and trumpets, as also with fumes of wine, to undergo valiantly the jousts of mutual love; you see their amorous frenzy, their hair flying in the wind; you note their sighs of longing, and how they piss with excitement. A prize is set, as in the feast of Pope Alexander VI, to be given to the most intrepid tribad: Laufeia calls upon the brothel-girls to let her ride them, and carries off the crown (39); there is none there of better heart than Medullina, expert in plying her loins and buttocks; there all

---

the water; thus collected it will spurt out with greater force."

(38) Verse 335-339.

"But all the Moors and Indians well know the flute-girl who showed a bigger penis than great Caesar's two anti-Catos, in that place from which a rat will fly, conscious of possessing testicles. . . ."

(39) The "nimble hips" are those of the tribad, who is riding another in the posture of Apuleius' Fotis, *Metamorph.* II, p. 122, when she gratified Lucius with the joys of a superincumbent Venus.

etiquette ceases, mistresses and servants alike
contest for the palm of obscenity; there is
no sham, all is tribadic reality (40); but,
after all, finally nature got the upper hand
again, the tribad disappeared, and the woman became again a woman, leaving alone
tribadism, as a phantom only of pleasure, and

---

(40) All this was actually represented in Paris, 1791,
on the stage of a theatre, where, according to the author
of the *Gynaeology* III, 423, a man completely naked had
connection with a woman as naked as himself, both
representing savages, accompanied by the plaudits of both
sexes. There is however nothing new under the sun.
With the Romans it had long been customary, after the
public games were finished, to bring prostitutes into the
arena, and set them to work, so that the spectators might
have an opportunity to perform what they had been
looking at with greedy eyes; a herald proclaimed what
was to come. Tertullian, *De Spectaculis,* ch. 17: "Prostitutes, the victims of public incontinence, are brought
upon the stage, shamefaced with respect to the women
only; to the men they were known; they are exposed to
the laughter of all, high and low; their dwellings, their
prices, even their recommendations were proclaimed by
the crier." Isidorus, *Origines,* XVIII, 42: "The theatre
is like a brothel; when the games are over, public women
are prostituted there." The rape of the Sabines described
in Livy (II, 18) would seem to have been a not dissimilar
form of amusement: "In this year young Sabines in Rome
having, in the midst of the games, abducted some prostitutes, the tumult ensuing thereupon degenerated into a
riot, in fact nearly into a battle."

not satisfying them; from all parts a cry is raised: "Now is the time for the men to come in: go and find young men; if you cannot find any, then slaves will do; if they are lacking, bring the first men you can find in the streets." And if all fails, in their shameless wantonness, they will offer their buttocks to an ass (41). On the origin of tribads (42) Phedrus has a fable, IV, 14:

"Another asked the reason why tribads and cinedes were created. The old man thus explained: The same Prometheus, modeller of the human clay, that if it knock against Fortune is shivered in pieces, once when he had been fashioning all day long separately those parts that modesty keeps hidden be-

---

(41) Observe the subtlety of the expression adopted by the poet: "offers her buttocks to an ass to get on them." Juvenal knows that a woman has no chance to have an ass's mentula in her except by turning her back to the beast.

(42) Plato, *Symposium* (Works, Zweibrücken edition, vol. X, p. 205) imagines another origin; in the passage where he relates the celebrated fable, according to which Jupiter had cut the men in halves, he says: "As to those women who are halves of women, they are not much harassed by desires after men; but are much more given to amuse themselves with women; the hetairistriae descend from their category."

neath a garment, to fit them presently to the bodies he had made, was unexpectedly invited to supper by Bacchus. There he imbibed the nectar in large drafts, and returned late home with unsteady foot; then what with fumes of wine and sleepiness, he joined the female parts to male bodies, and fixed male members on to the women. Thus it is we find lust indulging in depraved pleasures."

The masculine member applied to women is evidently that clitoris of such proportions in erection, that the tribads can use it like a penis; the female apparatus fitted on to man is nothing else but the posterior orifice, which itches in the case of cinedes, just as the vulva titillates women. Tribads were not wanting in the times of Tertullian; he calls them frictrices. *De Pallio,* ch. 4:

"Look at those she-wolves who make their bread by the general incontinence; amongst themselves they are also frictrices."

The same author says in the *De Resurrectione Carnis,* ch. 16: "I do not call a cup poisoned which has received the last sigh of a dying man; I give that name to one that has been infected by the breath of a frictrix, of a high-priest of Cybelé, of a gladiator, of an executioner, and I ask if you will not refuse it as you would such persons' actual kisses."

Nor was the trade of tribad out of date in the time of Aloysia Sigaea:

"Nay! do not think me", says Tullia, Dialogue II, "worse than others. This taste is spread almost over the universe. Italians, Spaniards, French, are all alike as to the tribadism of their women; if they were not ashamed, they would always be rutting in each other's arms."

More, she quotes herself some examples of the hot transports of tribads, Dialogue VII:

"Enemunda, the sister of Fernando Porcio, was very beautiful, and not less so was a friend of hers, Francisca Bellina. They frequently slept together in Fernando's house. Fernando laid secret snares for Francisca; the latter knew that he desired to have her, and was proud of it. One morning the young man, stung by his desires, rose with the sun, and stepped out upon the balcony to cool his hot blood. He heard the bed of his sister in the next room cracking and shaking. The door stood open; Venus had been kind to him and had made the girls careless. He enters; they do not see him, blinded and deafened by pleasure. Francisca was riding Enemunda, both naked, full gallop. 'The noblest and most powerful mentulas are every day after my maidenhead,' said Francisca, 'I should select the finest, dear, but for you; so fain am I to gratify your tastes and mine.' Whilst speaking she was jogging her vigorously. Fernando threw himself naked into the bed; the two girls, almost frightened to death, dared not stir. He draws Francisca, exhausted by her ride, into his arms and kisses her: 'How dare you, abandoned girl,' he says, 'violate my sister, who is so pure and chaste? You shall pay me for this; I will revenge the injury done to our house; answer now to my flames as she has answered to yours.' 'My brother! my brother!' cries Enemunda, 'pardon two lovers, and do not betray us to slander!' 'No one shall know anything,' he answered, 'let Francisca make me a present of her treasure, and I will make you both a present of my silence.''

The conversation of Ottavia with Tullia, acting as tribad, in the same work (Dialogue II) is still bolder and more to the point:

TULLIA: Pray do not draw back; open your thighs.

OTTAVIA: Very well! Now you cover me entirely, your mouth against mine, your breast against mine, your belly against mine; I will clasp you as you are clasping me.

TULLIA: Raise your legs, cross your thighs over mine, I will show you a new Venus; to you quite new. How nicely you obey! I wish I could command as well as you execute!

OTTAVIA: Ah! ah! my dear Tullia, my queen! how you push! how you wriggle! I wish those candles were out; I am ashamed there should be light to see how submissive I am.

TULLIA: Now mind what you are doing! when I push, do you rise to meet me; move your buttocks vigorously, as I move mine, and lift up as high as ever you can! Is your breath coming short?

OTTAVIA: You dislocate me with your violent pushing; you stifle me; I would not do it for any one but you.

TULLIA: Press me tightly, Ottavia, take
. . . there! I am all melting and burning, ah!
ah! ah!

OTTAVIA: Your affair is setting fire to mine
—draw back!

TULLIA: At last, my darling, I have served
you as a husband; you are my wife now!

OTTAVIA: I wish to heaven you were my
husband! What a loving wife I should make!
What a husband I should have! But you
have inundated my garden; I am all be-
dewed! What have you been doing, Tullia?

TULLIA: I have done everything up to the
end, and from the dark recesses of my vessel
love in blind transports has shot the liquor of
Venus into your maiden barque.

Leo Africanus, in his *Description of Africa,* p. 336 (edition Elzevir, of 1632), mentions the tribads of Fez:

"But those who have more common sense,
call these women (he is speaking of witches)
"Sahacat," a word which corresponds with
the Latin *fricatrices,* because they take their
pleasure with each other. I cannot speak
more plainly without offending decency.
When good-looking women visit them, these

witches fall at once in hot love with them, not less hot than the love of young men for girls, and they ask them in the guise of the devil to pay them by suffering their embraces. So it happens that very often when they think they have been obeying the behests of demons, they have really only had to do with witches. Many, too, pleased with the game they have played, seek of their own impulse to enjoy intercourse again with the witches, and under pretence of being ill, summon one of them or send their unfortunate husbands to fetch her. Then the witches, seeing how matters stand, asseverate that the wife is possessed by a demon, and can only be liberated by joining their association."

You ask whether tribads are still to be found in our days? If there are none now, there certainly were some in existence in Paris only a short time before the Great Revolution, if we are to trust the author of *Gynaeology,* III, p. 428. There was a veritable college of tribads in Paris, who went by the names of Vestals, holding regular meetings in particular localities. There were a great many members, and of the highest classes; they had their statutes with respect to admission; the affiliated were divided into three degrees: aspirants, postulants, the initiated. Before the postulant could be admitted to the secret of the order, she had to undergo for three days a difficult probation: shut up in a cell tapestried with lewd pictures, and ornamented with carved Priapi of magnificent proportions, she had to keep up a fire with I do not know how many ingredients, and arranged in such a manner that it would go out if there was taken too much or too little of any of the materials; on the four altars of the temple, which was adorned with statues of Sappho, of the Lesbians she had loved, and of the Chevalier d'Eon, who for so many years successfully dissimulated his sex, and with splendid hangings, perpetual fires were burning. Kept English women, too, did not recoil at tribadism, as the same author states, III, p. 394. He affirms that not long before the close of the last century, confederacies of tribads, called Alexandrine confederacies, were still in existence in London, though in a small number only.

Enough now of those who are, strictly speaking, included under the name of tribads; but the word has a more extended signification. The term is also applied to those women who in default of a real mentula, make use of their finger or of a leathern contrivance, which they introduce into their vulva, and so attain a fictitious enjoyment. Germany, I have lately heard, has been ringing with complaints about this abuse. As regards the leathern engine (43), called by the Greeks olisbos, the women of Miletus, above all others, made it their instrument of pleasure. Aristophanes, in the *Lysistrata,* 108-110:

"For since the day the Milesians left us in the lurch, not an olisbos have I set eyes on, eight inches long,—that might give us its leathern aid. . ."

Suidas under the word "****":

"A virile member made of leather which was used by Milesian women, as being tri-

---

(43) Another use of these leathern engines has been noted in chap. II.

bads and immodest.   It was also made use of by widows."

The same author under the word ****:

"Cratinus also says on this head: *Lewd* women will be using the olisbos."

Hesychius quotes the same passage:

If you ask whether modern women, who have suffered the wrong of seeing their beauty slighted, actually have recourse to this leathern substitute, Aloysia Sigaea (Dialogue II) shall answer you:

"The Milesian women made for themselves imitations in leather, eight inches long and thick in proportion.   Aristophanes tells us that the women of his day habitually made use of such.   And to this very day Italian, Spanish and Asiatic women honor this instrument with a place in their toilet apparatus; it is their most precious possession, and one very highly appreciated."

It is an undoubted fact that the Roman matrons cherished a species of inoffensive snake (44), the cold skin of which served

(44) This sort of snake served also to amuse men. Suetonius, *Tiberius,* ch. 72: "He kept for amusement a snake; one day, when he went as usual to feed it, he

as a refrigerator in summer, Martial, VII, 86:
"If Glacilla winds an icy serpent round
her neck . . ."

Lucian *Alexander* (Works, vol. IV, p. 259):
"In that country one sees serpents of an
enormous size, but so quiet and mild that they
are fondled by women, sleep with the children, do not get angry on being trodden on
or handled, and suck the nipples of the breast
like a nursling."

This being so, our eminent Bottiger was
probably right, when he wrote page 454 of
his *Sabina* (45) a profoundly scientific work
in German, that very likely snakes were used

---

found it devoured entirely by ants, which he took as a
warning to guard against being attacked by a mob."
Pliny, *Nat. Hist.* XXIX, ch. 4: "The Aesculapian serpent was brought to Rome from Epidaurus; it was kept
in the public edifices, and also in private houses." Seneca,
in the *De Ira,* II, ch. 31, speaks of: "Those snakes that
glide harmlessly amid the cups and into the bosoms of
the guests." They were not of a small size; this appears
from what Philostratus says in his *Heroics,* VIII, 1:
"Ajax had a tame snake of five cubits length, which kept
close to him, guided him on his way, and followed him
about like a dog." This kind of snake was very common
at Pella, in Macedonia, as Lucian says in a passage quoted
in the text: "There are many such in their country."
They are still to be found in Italy, according to Justus
Lipsius in his Notes to Seneca.

as instruments to satisfy the lubricity of amorous women. You may understand now what happened, or what might have happened to Atia, the mother of Augustus, of whom Suetonius (*Augustus,* ch. 94) wrote:

"I read in the treatise of Asclepiades of Mendé called the *Theologumena,* how Atia the mother of Augustus, having gone at midnight to the temple of Apollo, to assist at a solemn sacrifice, fell asleep, and so did the other women present; how a serpent suddenly glided close to her, and after some little time withdrew again, and how on waking she purified herself, as though she had left the arms of her husband."

There would be nothing surprising in the fact that a serpent of that sort should have investigated even without incitation on Atia's part, a certain locality which was well known to it by the lubricity of other women, and that Atia felt on awakening the very same sensation as though she had undergone a real coitus.

---

(45) "Sabina, or the Morning Toilette of a Roman Lady at the end of the First Century," translated into French by Clapier, 1813, 8vo.

CHAPTER VII

OF INTERCOURSE WITH ANIMALS

T will not be out of place to say something here of the incontinence of those who have carried out carnal intercourse with animals. It appears that in Egypt the Mendesians, who paid divine honors to a he-goat (46), prostituted to him publicly women, even against his inclination, in celebrating his rites. Herotodus II, 46:

"A monstrous affair was connected with this district (viz., the Mendesian) in my time; a he-goat covered a woman in public."

Strabo, XVII, p. 802:

"Mendes, where they worship Pan, and a

---

(46) Plutarch, *Of Animals that have Reason,* p. 989, vol. II, of his works: "It is reported in Egypt the he-goat Mendes, shut up with a great number of women, all of them beautiful, refused to have anything to do with them, and prefers goats by far."

live he-goat; the latter in that place have intercourse with women (47)."

The Jews also knew something of the practice; as we know from the law of Moses, Leviticus xx, 15-16:

"And if a man lie with a beast, he shall surely be put to death: and ye shall slay the beast. And if a woman approach unto any beast, and lie down thereto, thou shalt kill the woman, and the beast: they shall surely be put to death" . . .

How should Juvenal have come to tell us, Satire VI, 332-33:

". . . no more delay is there; she hastens to make a donkey ride her from behind," if it had not been known that women sometimes submitted themselves to asses? Would Apuleius have thought of describing to us with no less minuteness than wit the scene in which Lucius, changed into an ass by a mistake of Fotis, effects intercourse with a matron? *Metamorphoses,* book X, p. 249:

"But I was a prey to grave apprehensions;

---

(47) If we may believe Venette (II, iv. 3), there is nothing more common in Egypt at the present day than for young women to have intercourse with he-goats.

I asked myself how I, with my long and coarse legs, could mount a delicate woman, clasp with my hard hoofs her soft and tender limbs that looked like milk and honey; how could I with my enormous mouth, furnished with teeth as big as tomb-stones, kiss those small, rosy, scented lips; how lastly this lady, although in rut to her very finger nails, could take in such a big genital verge . . . She, however, doubled her tender allurements, her endless kisses, her sweet murmurings, interspersed with sweet glances like stings: 'I hold you at last,' she cried, 'I hold my dove, my sparrow!' and having said this, she showed me how vain my fears had been for embracing me as closely as she could, she received me inside entirely, out and out. Even more than that, whenever I drew back in order to spare her, she pushed closer to me, and clasping my backbone like mad, she clung to me so closely that, by Hercules, I began to think that I was not well enough furnished to assuage her passion completely."

A young girl of Tuscany got herself covered by a dog in the time of Pius V, the Roman Pope, as reported by Venette II, iv., ch. 3; and according to a note of Elmenhorst on the above quoted passage of Apuleius, a woman was discovered in Paris, in October, 1601, to have had connection with a dog. The law was appealed to, and in conformity with the unanimous verdict pronounced by the parliament, the adulterous woman and the dog were both burnt alive. Nay! more, a woman has been known to submit to a crocodile, if we may believe Plutarch, who reports in his treatise *On the Sagacity of Animals* (p. 976, vol. II, of the complete Works):

"Quite lately our excellent Philinus, on returning from a long voyage to Egypt, told me that he had seen at Antaeopolis an old woman sleeping with a crocodile stretched comfortably beside her on her pallet."

Nor have men despised the vulva of animals. Plate III of the *Monuments du Culte Secret des Dames Romaines,* shows the picture of a man working away in a goat, though the annotator ought not to have quoted in illustration of it a passage of Virgil (*Bucolics* III., 8.), which has nothing whatever to do with this matter:

"We know who (pedicated) you, while the he-goats looked at you askance."

In our countries legal cases show that not only goats, but also sheep, cows, and mares, have sometimes charmed shepherds and other people of low breeding.

CHAPTER VIII

OF SPINTRIAN POSTURES

IN the sundry kinds of voluptuous enjoyment which we have studied so far, there are almost always only two persons in action. It happens, nevertheless, that more than two, three or even more, may enjoy themselves together; this is what we call after Tiberius, the spintrian kind. Suetonius, *Tiberius,* ch. 43:

"In his retreat at Capri he had a *sellaria,* the scene of his secret debaucheries, in which chosen groups of young girls and worn-out voluptuaries, the inventors of monstrous conjunctions, called by him *spintries,* formed a triple chain, surrendered themselves to mutual defilements in his presence, so as to reanimate by this spectacle his languishing desires."

This *sellaria,* by the etymology of the word,

was evidently a room furnished with seats; those who prostituted each other on these seats were called *"sellarii,"* from the place, and *"spintriae,"* from the chain they formed. Spinter, according to Festus, p. 443, signified, "a kind of bracelet worn by women on the upper part of the left arm." The word is probably a corruption of *sphincter,* the Greek **** from ****, "I clasp," as for instance, a band surrounding the arm. Tacitus, *Annals,* VI., ch. 1:

"Then there were invented names never known before, as for instance, *sellarii* and *spintriae,* names taken from the turpitude of the place or from the complicated infamies undergone."

Spintries then are those who, linked like the rings of a bracelet, thus accomplish the pleasures of Venus. Three can link themselves thus, two and two, in such a way that while the middle one is a fornicator or a pedicon, in front is a woman or a cinede, behind a pedicon. Such was the chain formed

by those ausonius (*Epigram* **CXXIX.**) describes (48) :

"Three in one bed; two submit to the infamous act, two perform it.—Four there are,
I suppose.—Wrong! to the outermost ones
give a villainy apiece; count the man in the
middle twice, for he both acts and submits.

Do you want to see the one in the middle
working a woman?   Plate XL. of the *Mon-*
uments de la Vie Privée des douze Césars
shows you an example.   Do you wish to see
the middle one pedicating?   Look at plate
XXVII.

There is, however, no need that the middle
actor should fornicate or pedicate.   He may
be placed between his two companions in
such a way that while he is enduring the
assault of a pederast behind, he may in front
irrumate, suck a member or lick a vulva.
Hostius whose mind was so fertile in inventing
obscenities that he was held up as an example to future ages, has tried all these postures
and even added fresh variations.   Seneca
(Nat. Quaest., I., 16) has inveighed against

(48) Translation by Ausonius of a Greek Epigram of
Strata, to be found in Brunck's *Analecta*, II, 380.

him more vehemently than is perhaps fit for a philosopher. It seems to me as though some secret voluptuousness has been acting here on the sense of this rigid guardian of virtue; he says:

"I will tell you here a story which will show you that lust will not distain any artifice which is calculated to rouse desires, and to stimulate its own fury. The lasciviousness of Hostius was of the extremest kind. It was this rich miser, this slave of a hundred million sesterces, whose death, when he had been assassinated by his slaves, Augustus would not avenge, although he would not say that they were right to kill him. His lewdness was not contented with one sex; he was as passionate for men as for women. He had mirrors made which magnified the reflections so much that a finger appeared as big as an arm. These mirrors were placed in such a manner that when he had a man under him he could watch every movement of his accomplice, and enjoy as it were the fictitious size of his member. He chose his men carefully, the measuring tape in hand, and still had to deceive his insatiable passion.

It would be too outrageous to report everything which this monster, that ought to have been torn into pieces, dared to say and do with his mouth; when surrounded on all sides by his mirrors he was the spectator of his own turpitudes, and those secret infamies which every man would deny, if accused of them, of such he took his fill not with his mouth only, but also with eyes. And, by Hercules, generally speaking crimes shun their own reflection; men who are bare of every feeling of honor and exposed to every insult, still have some sense of shame, and do not appear as they are. But he feasted his eyes on unheard of and unknown infamies, and, not content to see simply how he dishonored himself, he surrounded himself with mirrors, for the sake of multiplying and grouping his lubricities. As he could not see unaided everything distinctly when, pedicated by one man, he had his head between the thighs of another, he saw by his mirrors what he was doing and how. He saw the lewd work of his mouth, and watched himself absorbing men by every orifice. Sometimes placed between a man and a woman,

playing both ways the passive part, he was
able to see the greatest abominations. Darkness was not for him! So far from being
afraid of the light of day, he wanted it for
his monstrous copulations, and was proud to
have them illuminated by it. Nay, more, he
even wanted to be painted in these attitudes.
Even prostitutes have a certain reserve, and
those that abandon themselves to the out-
rages of all, veil to some extent their poor
complaisances, and the very brothel keeps
some relics of decency; but this monster
turned his obscenities into a spectacle for
himself.

"Yes," he said, "I submit myself to a man
and a woman at the same time; but nevertheless with the organs which are left free to
me I am still able to commit a worse ig-
nominy. All my limbs are polluted; then
shall my eyes also take part in my enjoy-
ments, they shall be witnesses and judges.
What I cannot see in a natural way let me
see by the help of art, so that I may not be
ignorant of what I am doing. No matter
to me that Nature has provided man with
such insignificant organs of voluptuousness,

the same nature which has furnished animals so well; I find means to deceive my passion, and to satisfy myself. Where is the harm, if I try to imitate nature? I will have mirrors which shall reflect images of incredible dimensions. If I could, I would make these images real; as I cannot, I must be satisfied with phantoms. Let me see these objects of obscenity larger than they are in reality, and surprise myself by the sight of them!"

Plate XXI. of the *Monuments de la Vie Privée des douze Césars* shows the picture of Tiberius in a very strange spintrian posture, which, however, is not without charm; the emperor, half reclining on his back, licks one girl's privates who is kneeling over him, while he offers his penis to be sucked by another.

There are also arrangements where more than three can join, making thus a longer chain. Let a man put his member into a woman while both of them are being pedicated at the same time, and you have four people forming a triple chain, like those of Tiberius in the passage of Suetonius quoted above. Suppose then another pedicon on each end, and then you have a group of five, forming a quadruple interweaving. Martial, XII, 43:

"There are to be found novel figures of Love, such as the impassioned fornicator may try, such as experienced libertines perform and keep the secret of; how five can copulate in a group, how more still may be connected in a chain."

Look at Plate XXXVI. of the *Monuments de la Vie privée des douze Césars*, with a group of five copulators artistically diversified. Nero, lying face downwards, enters one girl who is on her back, at the same time licking the privates of another who is standing; he himself is being pedicated, while the girl standing also submits her behind to a pedicon. That such a chain may be extended infinitely, is self evident.

ENUMERATION

OF THE

EROTIC POSTURES

1. The man face downwards taking between his thighs the woman, who lies on her back with her legs stretched out straight.
2. The man face downwards taken between her thighs by the woman, who lies on her back with the legs apart.
3. The woman lying on her back taking only one leg of her cavalier between her thighs.
4. The woman lying on her back with her feet crossed over the loins of the man.
5. The woman lying on her back with one of her legs stretched out, and the other over the man's loins.
6. The woman lying on her back with the cavalier mounted on her with his back towards her face.

7. The woman lying on her back, with the cavalier mounted athwart her.

8. The man lying with the woman half couched on her side with the legs stretched out.

9. The man lying with the woman half couched on her side, one leg stretched out, the other one over the man's loins.

10. The woman half couched, the man mounted with his back to her.

11. The man on his knees, the woman on her back with her legs open.

12. The woman on her back with her legs resting on the man's loins, who is kneeling.

13. The woman on her back, one leg stretched out, the other one resting on the loins of the man, who is kneeling.

14. The woman on her back with her legs on the shoulders of the man, who is kneeling.

15. The woman on her back with one leg resting on the loins of the man, who

is on his knees, and the other one on his shoulder.

17. The man kneeling gets into the woman, who is in a sitting position with her thighs open.

18. The woman sitting with one leg stretched out, and the other resting on the loins of the man, who is kneeling.

19. The woman sitting, with her two legs resting on the loins of the kneeling man.

20. The woman sitting with one leg stretched out, and the other on the shoulder of her cavalier on his knees.

21. The woman sitting with her two legs on the shoulders of her cavalier on his knees.

22. The woman sitting, one of her legs on the shoulder of the man on his knees, the other one stretched out.

23. The man on his knees, the woman with her back to him.

24. The man on his back, the woman facing him.

25. The man on his back with the woman turning her back to him.

26. The man on his back, the woman athwart him.

27. The man on his back, with the woman lifted up.

28. The man sitting with the woman facing him.

29. The man sitting, the woman facing him, with her legs in the air.

30. The man sitting with the woman turning her back upon him.

31. Man and woman standing.

32. Man and woman standing, with one leg of man or the woman lifted up.

33. The man standing, with the woman on her back, her legs open.

34. The woman lying on her back, with her legs lifted on the loins of the man, who is standing.

35. The woman lying on her back, one leg stretched out and the other lifted on the loins of the man, who is standing.

36. The woman on her back, with her two legs on the shoulders of the man, who is standing.

37. The woman on her back, one leg stretched out and the other one on the shoulder of the man, who is standing.

38. The woman on her back, with one of her legs on the shoulder of the man, who is standing, the other over his loins.

39. The man standing, the woman half lying on her side.

40. The man standing, getting into the woman who is sitting with her legs open.

41. The man standing, getting into the woman sitting with her legs in the air.

42. The man standing, the woman sitting with one leg stretched out and the other one lifted up.

43. The man standing and the woman lifted up.

44. The woman lifted up, with her legs on the shoulders of the man, who is standing.

45. The man standing, the woman on her knees, with her back towards him.

46. The man standing, the woman crouching down, with her back towards him.

47. The man standing, the woman with her back towards him, the lower part of the body elevated, and the upper part resting on the bed.

48. The man standing, the woman turning her back to him with the lower part of the body artificially raised.

49. A man lying down and being pedicated.

50. A man pedicated standing.

51. A man on his knees being pedicated.

52. A man pedicated crouching down.

53. Irrumator lying down

54. Irrumator sitting.

55. Irrumator standing.

56. Irrumator kneeling.

57. Irrumator crouching.

58. Cunnilingue lying down.

59. Cunnilingue sitting.

60. Cunnilingue standing.

61. Cunnilingue kneeling.

62. Cunnilingue crouching.

63. Fellatrix and cunnilingue.

64. Masturbator.

65. The helping hand.

66. A third hand helping.

67. The finger helping.

68. The assistance of a leathern *godemiche*.
69. Coitus with a male animal.
70. Coitus with a female animal.
71. Tribad at work on a woman.
72. Tribad pedicating.
73. Three spintries: a fornicator pedicated.
74. Three spintries: a pederast pedicated.
75. Three spintries: a fellator being pedicated.
76. Three spintries: a fellator entering a woman.
77. Three spintries: a fellator pedicating.
78. Three spintries: a fellator irrumating.
79. Three spintries: a fellatrix entered by a man.
80. Three spintries: a fellatrix pedicated.
81. Three spintries: a fellatrix offers her vulva for licking.
82. Three spintries: a cunnilingue fornicating.
83. Three spintries: a cunnilingue pedicating.
84. Three spintries: a cunnilingue irrumates
85. Three spintries: a cunnilingue being pedicated.

86. Three spintries; a female cunnilingue is entered by a man.
87. Three spintries: a female cunnilingue is pedicated.
88. Four spintries forming a double chain.
89. Four spintries forming a triple chain.
90. Group of five copulators.

THE END

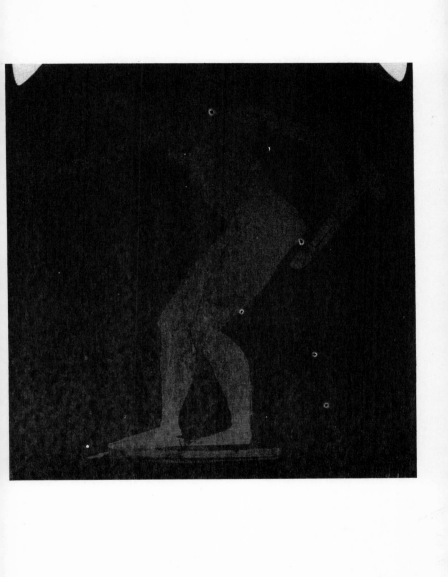